What "The Business" Says About Aggie Gold

"AGGIE GOLD is a persistent, untiring energetic fighter. Her clients do well in show business because Aggie never gives up."

— *Mark Upchurch, Talent Agent*
The Gilchrist Talent Group, Inc.

"The first manager that comes to mind is AGGIE GOLD. When the kids come into my office, you can tell they are with Aggie. They look well, act well and fit the part I've asked for. The parents speak highly of her. That is the tip-off, as parents are the gauge of how good a manager is. Her kids are just super. They are a pleasure to work with as well as Aggie. She's a real professional."

— *Mike Roscoe*
Mike Roscoe Casting

"AGGIE GOLD is an honest and caring manager of young talent."

— *Michelle Donay*
Michelle Donay Management

"Having worked with Aggie Gold for the past eight and a half years I've always found her to be very professional and ethical. She is a person who cares very much about her clients and their careers."

— *Barbara Coleman DiMarco, Head of Commer-*
cial Youth Division, J. M. Bloom & Associates

"When I started in this business six years ago, Fresh Faces Management (Aggie's company) was already an established management with a solid reputation. Aggie Gold stands behind each one of her clients, because they don't become her clients unless they meet her standards of excellence. In terms of her clients, Aggie's policy has always seemed to be 'QUALITY, NOT QUANTITY.'"

— *John Shea, Talent Agent*
  Schiffman, Ekman, Morrison & Marx, Inc.

"In a business as hectic and demanding as ours, it's nice to know that I can rely on such an efficient manager with a talented pool of clients. AGGIE GOLD is aggressive and a real go-getter! She knows talent. It is truly a joy to work with her."

— *Ayn Lauren, Talent Agent*
  Kronick Kelly Lauren Abrams Artists

"It has been a pleasure to work with AGGIE GOLD and her clients over the years. She is a tough fighter..."

— *Steve Goldstein, Theatrical General Manager*
  "M. Butterfly"

"AGGIE GOLD and I share a very deep concern for, and interest in, this country's children. Her book, FRESH FACES, reinforces the concepts I try to present to my students—set a goal, give it your best shot, and believe that you are special! I have no doubt that Aggie's book is going to be of both interest and value to her readers."

— *Harri Meyers, Teacher*
  Baldwin Senior High School

"I have known AGGIE GOLD as a co-worker, professional associate, and friend over the past five years. She is, in my estimation, a fine children's manager, extremely energetic, a creative mind and is able to spot talented young people. She and her company are aware of everything that is going on in the business and she has excellent rapport with her clients and their parents as well.

"Aggie is a hard worker and commits herself fully in all her endeavors. She is a supportive and loving friend, and is a pleasure to work with."

— *Adrienne Albert*
  Fox Albert Management Enterprises Inc.

"In working with Aggie Gold, I feel the children she manages are very dependable, very professional and quite successful in the New York commercial and Theatre industry. She is very personable and I would recommend her as a manager highly."

— *Lisa Abramovitz, Talent Agent*
  Frontier Booking International Inc.

Aggie Gold shares her experience with you in FRESH FACES, the only book you need to help your child break into any area of show business.

FRESH FACES

GETTING YOUR CHILD INTO COMMERCIALS, TELEVISION AND THE MOVIES

By Aggie Gold

THE CAREER PRESS
62 BEVERLY RD.,
PO BOX 34
HAWTHORNE, NJ 07507
1-800-CAREER-1
201-427-0229 (OUTSIDE U.S.)
FAX: 201-427-2037

FRESH FACES Getting Your Child Into Commercials, Television And The Movies
ISBN 0-934829-72-1, $10.95

Cover photographs courtesy of Jean Elizabeth Poli Photography, New York, NY

Cover Design by Harvey Kraft, Maher & Partners

Copies of this volume may be ordered by mail, FAX phone directly from the publisher.

To order by mail, please include price as noted above, $2.50 handling per order, plus $1.00 for each book ordered. Send to: The Career Press Inc., 62 Beverly Rd., PO Box 34, Hawthorne, NJ 07507.

FAX your order: 201-427-2037.

Or call Toll-Free 1-800-CAREER-1 (in Canada: 201-427-0229) to order using your VISA or Mastercard or for further information on all books published or distributed by The Career Press.

Table of Contents

Action!
The Contacts You Need To Succeed

Introduction

You Ought To Be In Pictures

People stop you in the street. At the supermarket. At the dry cleaners. "Wow," they say, "Your child is *so* cute. Did I just see her on a 'Burger King' commercial? What? Your child isn't *on* television? Why *not?*"

The local department store photographer thinks Benjamin could start modeling tomorrow. The hairdresser is convinced Lindsay could be another Shirley T. And, of course, your entire bridge club is absolutely convinced *your* little Tiffany could easily become the next *Tiffany*.

You're certainly not immune to your pride and joy's charms. So photogenic! So expressive! So gosh darned cute. You think about the times he has entertained family and friends by singing his favorite song or acting out his favorite story—heroically playing the caped crusader slaying the dragon and saving the maiden.

Maybe your child has even "felt the calling" and, while watching a group of kids cavort across a lawn extolling some toothpaste's secret ingredient or a cereal's potent sugar coating, told you right out, "Mom, I want to do that."

As your child tells you this more often, as you see with your own eyes how talented she seems to be, as more and more other people—heck, total strangers—walk up to you just to comment on your kid's hair, or skin, or smile, or just general gorgeousness, you can't help thinking the same thing every time *you* see those kids in that toothpaste ad: *That could be my kid!*

But then you get a double attack of "objectivity" and "reality" and tell yourself, "Who am I kidding? Those kids are trained actors. Sure they make lots of money, but obviously they sing and dance and act a lot better than Jason (or Jennifer or Jeremy or...). They live in Hollywood. And they've got connections I could never get—like an uncle that just happens to own a movie studio. It's all who you know out there. Jason (or...) wouldn't stand a chance."

I've got news for you. Connections—at least connections like that—have nothing to do with it.

And your child doesn't have to be the embodiment of the Gerber baby. And able to sing like Judy Garland, dance like Fred Astaire, and act like Sir Lawrence Olivier.

If your child wants to act in commercials, TV, the theater or movies—and if you want him or her to do it and are ready as parents to make the sacrifices and do the work necessary to make it happen—it *can* happen.

It happens every single day...to kids exactly *like* Jason and Jennifer and Jeremy.

Within months, your child *could* very well be the one in the toothpaste ad.

Being shy. Wearing braces. Even lisping.

And this book will show you exactly how to do it.

Did I Get Your Attention?

I've been a personal manager representing children for over ten years. And most of my clients are children you would probably recognize from television commercials, soap operas, and major motion pictures.

The parents of these now highly successful kids were just as uninformed, just as scared, just as ready to "write off" show business for their kids as you might be—because they couldn't believe their kids really had a chance either. I remember the mothers and fathers asking me, "Do you think my child will ever make a *commercial?* Do you think my child will ever be in a *movie?* Do you think my child will ever *work?*"

I used to look at them and say, "You know, one day you're going turn on the television and every time you switch channels, your child is going to be in a commercial. You're going to be so used to seeing your kid on television you won't give her a second glance. But even better, one day you'll look at your child's bank account and realize not only is *her* college paid for, but so is college for your other two kids—and your child-actor is only *six!.*"

I guess it *is* very hard to believe that your child *can* actually work on television, be in a soap opera, star in a movie, model the latest fashions—or that your child could have college paid for by the time he or she is 6 or 7 or 10 years old.

It can happen, and it does happen. Over and over again! *It's not really that difficult.* What it takes is a positive attitude, patience, persistence, and taking advice from one who knows —me. Which is why you bought this book!

Here's How We're Going To Do It

Yes, this book is expressly written for those parents who want to get their children into show business and don't know how. As such, it is a "how to" manual—you don't need to bring any talent or preparation or research to the table; just read the book. And I hope it helps you get your child into this lucrative and exciting industry. Show business may not be for everyone, but if you can handle the pace, it can be an exciting and rewarding experience for both you and your child.

Avoiding The Rip Offs

But there's another reason I feel this book is essential. I've interviewed thousands of children and their parents, and heard every detail of their trek towards Hollywood-Mecca... and all the potholes they've run into along the way. And I'm still amazed how often parents are ripped off...and how angry I still get when I hear one more sleazy story. But there are just too many horror stories of parents spending hundreds, even thousands of dollars...and getting nothing for their money but a set of bad photographs.

Many of you have probably been contacted at one time or another by a company claiming to have heard about how beautiful your child is. Perhaps they claimed your child was recommended to them by someone. They stress how talented they've heard your child was. How beautiful. How poised!

If you haven't, here's how it works: By letter or phone, they'll ask you to set up an appointment and come in to meet with them. (And, by the way, they probably didn't get a referral from a local talent agency, producer or manager—unless you count birth announcements in the local paper as "referrals.") When you bring your child into their office, everybody you meet will just be full of superlatives: "Wow, your child is so wonderful! Your child is so beautiful! Your child is so talented!"

All you to have to do is give them anywhere from a couple of hundred dollars to a couple of thousand for pictures, acting classes, and dancing lessons, and then you're set! And it seems like such a reasonable investment—Isn't your child worth it? *Don't you want your child to succeed?? **Don't you want your child to make absolute oodles of money???***

Met Any Dinosaurs Lately?

Well, let's clear this up right away. First of all, nobody can *promise* you *any*thing. Guarantees are like dinosaurs—they don't exist. And certainly nobody can promise you that your child will become a *star* or make more money than the average Savings & Loan has lost. Whether your Michael can become the next "Mikey" is up to you and your child and no one else. The only *real* promises in this business are those made by the managers and agents who will wind up representing your child—**that they will work their hardest to help promote your child's career.** That's it. Anyone who promises to do more—no matter how sincere they seem and especially if they require up-front money to wave their magic wands—is not out to help *you,* just their bank accounts.

You can easily locate other rip-offs in your local newspaper, which probably has one or more ads from companies calling themselves "modeling agencies" or "talent representatives," announcing that they are looking for new faces for commercials and major motion pictures. When you take your child to one of these companies, it's the same story—you are told you need professional pictures, which, of course, they will be happy to "shoot" for you...for another $1,000 or so. The end result is always the same—another starry-eyed parent becomes a bit wiser and a lot more wary of the "show biz" jungle.

What these people are doing is *not* show biz! It's just another con game. So let me repeat the first important lesson you must tattoo on your arm: There are no promises worth listening to and there are no guarantees worth counting on in this business.

You alone control how far your child will get in this industry. Who you select to represent your child and your willingness to make the time, energy and financial sacrifices necessary to get your child into show business *the right way* are the only limiting factors.

(I will address both your own necessary preparations—making time, figuring costs, dealing with your children's schoolwork while they audition, etc. —and the correct way to choose a good representative in the first section of this book.)

How badly can being taken in by such con artists affect your attitude and chances?

One little girl—currently one of my top clients—was taken advantage of by one of these companies when she was four years old. Her mother had gone to somebody who claimed they were managers. They charged her tremendous fees for pictures. By the time the pictures were developed, they didn't even look like the little child.

But it wouldn't have mattered if they were the greatest pictures since Ansel Adams—the child never went out on auditions, because she was lost among the thousands of *other* bad pictures these charlatans had taken of previous victims!

So this little girl stayed on this management company's "roster" for almost two years, never doing anything, never sent anywhere. The mother constantly hoped that one day they would call. They didn't.

So she called them. And every time she did, got the same smooth excuse, "We're very sorry, but there isn't any work for your child's age range right now. We'll call you soon."

She finally was referred to me. I took one look at this little girl and said to myself, this kid has what it takes. She was so adorable, so outgoing, so cute. She didn't *need* pictures.

Within *two weeks,* she had three commercials on the air.

Yes, There's A Right Way, Virginia

I wrote this book because I want this dream to come true for *your* family, and I *know* it does *not* have to be a bad experience. But the odds are stacked against you—there are so many crooks out there! They pose as photographers. They pose as managers. They pose as agents. They pose as hot shot Hollywood producers. They come in all different sizes, shapes and colors. This book, I hope, will help put an end to all the misconceptions and the illegal dealings by giving you a clear picture of what is involved in getting your children into show business, legitimately...and *inexpensively.*

There is a right way to go about all this. **There is a legitimate, inexpensive, correct way of getting your child into show business.** It *doesn't* have to cost a lot of money, and it *doesn't* have to be a bad experience. And this book will show you exactly what you need to know, how to go about it, what to do, what not to do, who to trust, who not to trust, etc.

There are some good reasons why you should consider doing so, even if you've gotten this book as a gift and had never thought of getting your child into show biz. The children that work in this industry do extremely well, not only financially, but in school and in life—they develop into good, all-around kids. Their reading levels increase because they are always reading and have to memorize.

They also build self-confidence. When there is an audition, the parents are usually left in the reception area and the child is taken into a room with a casting director, a cameraman, maybe a producer or two, and then asked to say his lines for the audition. Imagine the confidence and poise necessary for a child to do that!

In one instance, one of my clients, a little six-year old girl, was asked to audition for ABC. Just before the audition, the casting director asked the mother, "Would you like to sit in on the audition?" The mother was thrilled because she had never really seen her daughter audition. So she sat quietly in a corner of the room while her daughter was led in front of six of the biggest brass at ABC. After the little girl was instructed to say her lines, she was asked several questions about herself. When the audition was finished, she stood up and (keep in mind, she's 6 years old) went over to each person, shook their hand, and said, "It was a pleasure meeting you."

The mother said to me afterwards, "You know, I was so nervous for her. I'm sitting there and I'm thinking, 'My god, the president of ABC, the head of casting, this producer, that director, and my daughter, full of confidence, went over to everybody, shook their hand, and spoke to them as if she had known them all her life.

"And it was no big deal to her.'"

The truth of the matter is, *it is no big deal.* This little girl may not stay in show business the rest of her life, but when she finishes college, applies for a job, and meets the president of a huge corporation, it's going to be no big deal to her. She's already met the head of network casting! She's so used to meeting people in very important situations that this is not going to faze her at all. The skills and poise that these children learn from show business will be essential skills they will utilize throughout their lives, even if they leave show business (as so many of them will).

So What's Normal?

Some people may feel that this business is not a normal life for a child—what with the stress of auditions, the distractions of missing school and traveling, the temptations of money and fame. If you define "normal" as a predictable routine of school and home and an occasional extracurricular activity, then this business is absolutely *not* normal.

But some kids are *happier* reading a script on a soap opera set than they are playing ball—a choice parents should allow their children to make. Kids in this business learn the same lessons taught by participation in sports or clubs—how to interact with adults, discipline, responsibility. And they learn these things, to a great extent, at a higher level than they would in school. Aside from that, they may well be earning lots of money while they learn—and I don't know of *any* school out there paying *students* for learning anything!

I'm in this business because I love to watch the growth—not only do I see children become successful and secure their financial futures (sometimes before they're able to *spell* F-I-N-A-N-C-I-A-L), but I watch their lives, and their parents lives, just get better and better.

I love what I do, with a passion. I love children. I get tremendous satisfaction finding a child who has the potential to be successful and helping him or her to achieve it.

As you read this book, I hope I can extend the same "helping hand" to those of you I will never be able to meet face-to-face.

As we say in the business, "Break a leg!"

Section One

Lights!

Essential Preparation

Chapter
1

What The Industry Is Looking For

Before we even talk about how your child looks and what "types" the industry is looking for, I'd like to give you an overview of the relative amounts of work available for children in each age group.

Oooh, Baby

The babies who usually work in commercials, television and movies are extremely easy-to-handle babies with great temperaments. They go easily from person to person without hesitation and with a minimum of fussing. They are predictable—with a regular nap and eating schedule—are not intimidated by a crowd, and can go into another room and leave their mothers behind with a minimum of fuss and bother.

These babies smile easily and are bright and alert. That's really it. It's a "good" baby that works in this business.

The competition is far stiffer for babies than it is for other children because baby calls are often "cattle calls"—hundreds of babies and their star-struck parents show up. At such an "audition," the casting director, who screens everybody, puts a lot of babies on videotape. Then she narrows it down to a handful of kids and presents them to the sponsor. If she sees 100 babies, maybe she'll present 25 to the sponsor. Out of 25, the sponsor will pick ten to use in the commercial. (Although they may only be using one in the commercial, because babies are so unpredictable, they'll have others around just in case.)

Given these odds, it's very, very difficult to get your baby into a commercial. That said, though, it's only fair to point out that it *can* be very easy, especially if you have a good baby. That's all they're looking for.

Beware The Terrible Twos

For children between the ages of two and three it is some-times harder still to find opportunities for work. Although every child does not go through the "Terrible Twos," the feel-ing in the industry is that children at this particular age are too unpredictable to count on. Most casting directors would rather use a child that is four, but *looks* two or three—their attention span is longer and they have a better understanding of what is going on and what is expected of them.

Where It's Happening

I would say that the hottest ages for commercials are children between four and ten. *There is really no particular type they're looking for.* Just as long as the child is natural and easy going. Most of my clients are in this age range.

Turn on the TV and look at some commercials. You'll quickly verify that most of the kids are in this age range, but you'll also notice that these children are all sizes, all colors, all shapes, some with missing teeth, some with all their teeth. In other words, kids just like yours!

It really doesn't matter to the people paying for the commercials. What really grabs the sponsor is a kid that can sell the product, which means a kid that is outgoing, verbal, and takes direction well. These are skills that you can develop in your child.

When Things Get Awkward

Between the ages of eleven and fourteen, children generally start going through puberty, which means pimples, braces, wild changes in voices, and, in general, awkwardness and gawkiness. Given this overwhelming hormonal attack, it is not surprising that many child actors, even the most successful, have to put their show business careers on hold during this period.

Because of these normal changes, boys and girls from ten to fourteen are used in a very limited way. They can no longer be considered children because they have started to develop, yet they can't be considered young adults because they are not fully developed. But don't get discouraged. There are a lot of kids in this age range who *are* working. And puberty eventually ends, transforming many a caterpillar into a butterfly.

My own daughter was very busy and worked quite a bit as a youngster. Then, when she started going through puberty, we had to put her career on hold for a while. It was disappointing to her because she missed it.

Happily, she's now fourteen, her braces are off, she has turned into a beautiful young lady, and she's starting to audition and work again. It happens.

Here's The Good News

Once children go through puberty, the market opens up again. As hot as the ages between four and nine are, children between fifteen and nineteen are hotter. Teenagers in all sizes and all colors and all shapes. It really makes no difference. Statistically teenagers buy vast amounts of products sold in this country, from clothing and cosmetics to food and records. It's not surprising that sponsors want representative teenagers "hawking" products their peers buy in such abundance.

This period is easier on parents, too—your children are pretty much old enough to go on auditions themselves and, if necessary, get part-time jobs to pay for any acting training that they wish to have.

Is There "A Look?"

For a very long time the only kids who worked were the gorgeous, "all American" ones—blond-haired, blue-eyed gods and goddesses with perfect teeth. But attitudes have changed.

Today, advertisers use and want children from all different ethnic backgrounds. They don't have to be gorgeous. In fact, they should look *average*. They want *regular* kids. Just turn on your television. Most of the kids you see in commercials or on television are just average, everyday kids. Just like yours.

Given that good news, there are still some important things you need to know about your child's physical appearance to make his entry into the business as easy as possible.

Smile For The Camera

Yes, children's teeth should be straight. Many children's commercials involve food, requiring the kids to eat, bite, chew. Any child hoping for such a commercial should have teeth that are clean and white, with no discoloration.

But there are exceptions to any rule. Just because your child doesn't have perfect teeth doesn't mean he doesn't have a chance to make it in this business.

I recently booked a Burger King commercial for a client of mine. I'm sure you know the commercial because her face is in the camera through its entirety—and it's hard *not* to notice that she's got two front teeth missing!

What happens when kids start losing their teeth? Some casting directors will suddenly start *requesting* them!

Others may prefer children with teeth for a particular commercial, but since they know how easy it is to correct the problem, they don't even hold it against the child without a tooth or two.

(The industry generally uses a *flipper*—a tiny bite plate with a fake tooth attached to it that children can just plop in their mouths; it fits in the space where they lost their teeth. As the tooth grows down, the fake tooth can be filed down so there is always a constant tooth.

If you ever walk into an audition room, you'll see all the little six-year olds taking out their flippers and showing them to each other.)

What About Braces?

Braces usually are not much in demand.

Yes, there are commercials that use children with braces, just as there are commercials that use children without teeth. The need for braces usually corresponds with the attack of puberty, so, in a way, it's good that all that happens at one time.

I would not suggest investing in professional pictures for a child with braces. I would wait until the braces come off.

No Pink Hair, Please

Children's hair should always be clean, shiny, and nicely styled, and *not* in a "trendy" cut or style. If your child insists on keeping his hair cut in the latest craze, then the roles that he will be considered for will be very limited. Don't pressure or force your child to cut his or her hair. Pressure never works with kids.

If he or she wants to work in the industry, your child will soon learn that hair teased to the ceiling or cut to the scalp will not help them get work. The first time they walk into a casting director's office, he or she will say, "If you don't change your hair style, there's not going to be much work for you." Leave it for the professionals to teach this lesson.

If your child wants to work, he or she will get the message...pronto.

Of Mice And Men

Pursuing a career in show business is probably the one time when a child who is small for his age has an *advantage*.

Children who are small for their age can get away with playing younger roles.

If your child is tiny, he or she may be very self-conscious about it. Just make sure you let him or her know that in *this* business being smaller is more desirable than anything else.

Why? Because a child that is small for his or her age is *always* preferred—they are brighter, their attention span is longer, they can work longer hours (by law), and they can usually take direction better. Children that are small for their age often do extremely well.

That's not to say that if you're *big* for your age you're not going to work.

I have a client who is so big for her age that everyone discouraged her. Meanwhile, this child is booking roles that are two years older than she is—she's seven years old and playing eight- and nine-year-old roles. She has been in the industry since she was an infant and is very professional. This is much more important to the directors who hire her than her age/size ratio!

It's important here to repeat a lesson learned earlier: If you have a highly motivated child, and you keep the child interested, there is no reason in the world why your child should not work. Whether they're big for their age, small for their age, average for their age. Short-haired. Long-haired. Gorgeous. Cute. Average. The working child and the successful child is the one who has extremely supportive parents, who has a desire to do this, and who can take direction well. And that's really it.

There's Room For Everybody

If you have a child who is handicapped, and he wants to break into this lucrative industry, I would not discourage him. More and more doors are being opened every day for these children, and more opportunities are being created for them. There is a place in show business for everybody.

As long as they want it, they can succeed. It's having that posi-tive attitude that will help achieve success.

But "Mumbles" Might Not Make It

Have you ever met a child who is very little, but who spoke like an adult? Well, that's very impressive, and that's what advertisers like. The smaller you are and the clearer you speak, the more opportunities there are for you.

"Mumbles" might have been a cute role for Dustin Hoffman in *Dick Tracy,* but he wouldn't get a lot of commercial work! Children have to speak clearly. Many times I interview adorable four-year-old children who just cannot be understood. They have all the characteristics I look for, but they don't speak clearly.

That's not to say they can't work until they can orate like the late Richard Burton. There are lots of commercials for little ones that don't require them to speak at all—they just have to sit there, look adorable, and hold the product. If your child cannot be understood, those are the type of jobs he or she should be auditioning for now. (Sometimes they even use children with lisps.) The important thing is to get the child working in whatever way and whatever format he or she can currently handle. When he or she starts talking like a champ, the experience will help land even better commercials and roles.

While you wait for nature to takes its course, there are things you can do with your children to help them overcome these speech difficulties. If they have trouble saying certain words, work with them. Practice them. They will eventually learn how to speak very clearly. In the meantime, they could be working and they could be making money.

Remember: No matter what—your kid's too big, too small, has too few teeth, can't talk well, needs glasses, whatever—don't close this book and don't get discouraged. Read on.

Nothing can hold you back and nothing can hold your child back unless *you* do.

Your child can be just as successful and make just as much money as any other kid on the tube.

Every time you turn on the television, you see the same children over and over again in the commercials. That could be your child. Very easily! It is *not* an unattainable dream. It could very easily be a reality for your family.

Chapter 2

'Cause You've Got Personality

I could walk into the reception area of a casting department and tell you, just by watching for a couple of minutes,
who is already successfully working in this business...and
who never will.

Let me show you how casting directors think by looking in
on a hypothetical office with two waiting rooms, A and B.

In Room A are teenagers waiting to audition for a new
motion picture. Over in one corner is Jill, a sixteen-year-old,
blue-eyed blonde—garishly over-dressed, wearing high heels
and heavy make-up. She seems to be more interested in fixing
her hair than in looking over the scene she's supposed to read
in five minutes.

In walks Mark, a seventeen-year-old who has arrived
more than twenty minutes late. He is disheveled, unorga-
nized, unprepared, and looking for an ashtray in which to

extinguish his cigarette. (By the way, an actor should never walk into an audition smoking.) He hasn't even had the courtesy to phone ahead to say he will be arriving late. Although Mark displays a warm and friendly personality, rather than beginning to concentrate on the audition he (thinks he) will be reading for, he is more interested in finding out what auditions everyone else has been on recently.

Near the door is Peggy, an attractive fifteen-year-old brunette, who is wearing blue jeans, a tailored blouse, vest and sneakers. She arrived ten minutes early to have time to study her scene. She has it memorized and is ready to go.

Ms. Albert, the casting director, enters the room and says, "Jill, you're next." Realizing she hasn't even glanced at the script, Jill asks for more time. This, of course, is impossible —appointments have been scheduled every ten minutes. The casting director tells her she must go now or forfeit her audition.

She needn't bother to read.

The casting director has *already* decided that Jill is an undisciplined actress who would not work out. Besides, she looks much older than her age. Not only has Jill not gotten this part, she has seriously hurt her chances of being seen by this particular casting director again...ever.

Having arrived late, without any prior notice, Mark, of course, has automatically forfeited his appointment. Ms. Albert, adding appearance to lateness, tells herself she will call Mark for another audition the instant she calls Jill.

When it is her turn, Peggy is prepared and ready to go in and give it her "best shot." The casting director is also anxious to have Peggy read—she is poised, well groomed, and has an air of confidence about her.

Ms. Albert has already made a mental note that if Peggy is not right for this part, she will surely keep her in mind for any future projects she may be casting.

At the same time that the fates of Jill, Mark and Peggy have been decided, Room B is filling with three- to six-year-old boys and girls ready to audition for a toy commercial.

Sherry, a pretty little five-year-old, is sitting very demurely next to her mother, who is nervously primping and fussing over her daughter's appearance.

At the opposite end of the room, Jack, a rambunctious, dark-haired six-year-old, is zooming around like a jet liner.

In the middle of the room are Jamie and Kelly, identical four-year-old twin girls. Both are coloring and inviting the other children to share their crayons and paper.

The twins approach Ms. Green, the casting director, as she enters the room. They show her their pictures and tell her about their day. Ms. Green is very receptive to the children, knowing that when it's their turn to audition, she'll remember them as two friendly, outgoing girls.

Out of the corner of her eye she sees Jack, still zooming around the room. Her immediate reaction—here's a child who could never adjust to a disciplined eight-hour commercial shoot with long periods of waiting and many retakes.

Sherry, still being fussed over by her mother, is barely noticeable when Ms. Green comes out to call her in. In fact, she needs coaxing to even go into the audition room.

It's Simpler Than You Think

What did Peggy, Jamie and Kelly have in common?

They are all bright, well-mannered, excited about being in an audition, and have the desire to be in show business—and *show* it in their appearance, behavior and preparation.

Their behavior towards the casting director shows that they will be able to work well with the other actors and technicians involved in a long tedious commercial or film shoot.

Aside from having good dispositions and outgoing personalities, there are many other criteria which must be met by
your child in order to succeed in this business. Your child:

- Must always be well groomed.
- Should never go to an audition dressed in the latest trendy fashions. Glitter stockings and wild
  outfits have no place at an audition.
- Should have no trace of a regional accent.
- Should be able to read well, or at least memorize.
- Must take direction well, and be willing and able
  to re-shoot scenes over and over again, giving his
  or her best performance each time.
- And most importantly, your child must do well
  in school. The children and teenagers who are
  successful in this industry are bright, energetic,
  ambitious, and usually at or near the top of their
  classes. These qualities make it possible to with-
  stand the demands of a full schedule of auditions
  and school work. (More on the importance of
  education and dealing with the pressures of
  school vs. work in chapter 5.)

Beauty, age, size and type are all certainly important, but
within each category is a wide range of acceptability. There is
no "best age" or "best size." It depends on what the casting
director is looking for to fill the specifications of the role she is
casting.

Does Your Child Have What It Takes?

How can you evaluate the suitability of *your* child's
personality for a career in show business?

In this business, your child will be called upon to perform
over and over again in front of people he's never met before.

That's not a difficult concept to convey to your child. In fact, you can practice that at home—get your child used to performing in front of everybody, whether it's grandma and grandpa, aunt and uncle, or the grocer and postman.

An outgoing, easy-going personality is essential. He should be willing to perform in front of anybody. Remember, keep it fun. Make it a fantasy for your child. It's play-acting. Children do this all the time and, for them, it's just make-believe.

Whatever you do and however you do it, get him used to it so when he goes in for an audition he's not going to hesitate about performing in front of a stranger. (More on this in the next chapter.)

It would be great if your child was outgoing all the time, but there are a lot of shy (and successful) children in this business, so being Little Mr. Personality is certainly not a prerequisite. And, from my experience, casting directors are very in tune with children and will usually give them a chance—when a shy child walks into a room, the casting director is not going to throw that child out. That child will get the same opportunity to say the lines, give the emotion, or perform whatever that casting director is looking for. Shy children often come to life when they're given something to say. Don't feel that if your child is not outgoing he doesn't have a chance. He definitely does.

Your child should be comfortable meeting new people. Some children are not, but that is something you can work on. It's funny, because in this crazy world that we live in, we teach our children *not* to talk to strangers and not to lie. Yet when we enter this business, we tell—heck, encourage—our children to talk to strangers. And though we don't encourage them to lie, we do kind of tell them to stretch the truth—if they are five and a half, for example, we tell them to say they are six years old.

Years ago, there was a major motion picture being cast with a key role for for a chubby, fourteen-year-old redhead. Now, I represented a chubby *thirteen*-year-old redhead who was a little bit big for his age. We got the script, and we worked on the role. I thought he was wonderful. He handled himself beautifully, and I felt he had an excellent chance at booking the role.

When he went for the audition, he did so well that he got a callback. At the callback he was told over and over again, "Gee, if you were only fourteen, if you were only fourteen." That was very frustrating for me, as his manager, and for him, because if he had gone into the audition and said he was fourteen instead of thirteen, he may have gotten the role. We'll never know.

As a personal manager for many years, I know when a ten-year-old child looks and behaves like an eight-year-old. Though I am not suggesting *you* try this—if you do, it could wind up backfiring in your face—if there is a role out there, I will let the casting director know that I am suggesting a child who is ten-years-old but looks and acts eight, and that I am going to send the child in and have the child *say* he or she is eight years old.

Now *that* is stretching the truth!

Chapter
3

Is Your Child Ready?

If your child is old enough to know what he or she wants, what he or she likes and dislikes, you will *never* be able to force him or her into a career in show business. If you do everything in your power to make it seem interesting and exciting, to point out the toys and other things their earned money can buy, and little "Tiffany Two" prefers to go play in the sandbox, you'd better start dreaming another dream. You may be motivated, but without your child being motivated, it is virtually impossible that he or she could ever succeed in this business. There are simply far too many highly motivated children out there already!

However, younger children aren't necessarily aware of all the ins and outs of show biz. If they perceive the auditions and shoots as entertaining games, it's quite possible they will learn to enjoy what they're doing without fully appreciating exactly what it is. And even older children, who might not have thought of the possibility of themselves being on television, can be brought around to the idea of "trying a tryout."

So let's presume you think your child, of whatever age, is a natural. What can you do to make the idea of a career in show business exciting to him or her?

Let's See What's On TV!

Find a nice comfortable spot to sit in—an easy chair, maybe the kitchen table after you've had breakfast. Call your child over and have him sit down with you. Maybe you'd like to make him a glass of chocolate milk or something that he likes. Make sure it's at a time when nobody else is going to disturb you. This should be a time for just you and your child.

Get your child very comfortable, perhaps even to the point of giggling. Talk about fun things. Talk about vacations.

When your child is relaxed and you judge the time is right, bring up the subject of television. Talk to him about his favorite programs and the children he can identify on these shows. Can he remember any particular commercials? Does he know any jingles? How does he feel about the other children on television? Does he think being on TV would be fun?

Turn the TV on and flip around the channels until you get to some children's programs. (The best time to really get a good idea of children's programming and commercials with lots of children in them is Saturday mornings on ABC, NBC and CBS—the three major networks. Many children watch television during those times and they probably know every commercial on the air by heart.) See if your child can sing along with the commercials or act along with the programs.

Say to your child, "Let's play acting. Can you say 'I feel very lonely?'" Have your child put on a real sad face and see if he can say the line with expression.

Or say, "Let's make believe you're happy, because we're going to McDonald's. I want you to say, 'Mom, I'm going to McDonald's!'" Have him stand up, jump up and down, wave his hands, really show some energy. If you don't think that's going to get him excited (it may not; he may *hate* McDonald's), choose some other place—a favorite restaurant, park, attraction, whatever. The idea is to get your child to show you "happy"—an emotion he will need often when he auditions—*on command.*

Put On A Face...Any Face

Try other emotions. For example, if you have a pet, make your child pretend that she can't find the pet. Let her show worry and sadness. If you don't have a pet, get your child to pretend that you do (let's call it Floppy the dog) and then do the same exercise. You might say to your child, "Now I want you to make believe we can't find Floppy. I want you to get very sad and show me a very sad face. If you want to rub your eyes and make believe you're crying, that's okay." Ask her to say, "I can't find Floppy" while she's pretend-crying.

Think of an incident which recently happened to your child and got him very angry. "Do you remember how angry you got at Billy for breaking your toy?" When he is able to "re-create" that feeling of anger, get him to say the line, "Billy broke my toy."

If you can't think of an incident that recently got your child angry, make up a story. Give him an example. Say to him, "What if your sister scribbled all over your pretty picture?" Ask him to say, "Susie ruined my picture." Make sure he's angry.

Pick up a magazine with lots of advertisements. Pick any advertisement—most of them are just one-liners—and have your child repeat it after you. Go over to a mirror with your child. Have him look at the mirror and say the different lines with the different emotions right into the mirror. Make it fun. Make it a game.

Pick out things on the television that you can ask your child to mimic. Talk to him about being on television and doing commercials. Remember: Children are the greatest natural mimics on the face of the earth. And acting really is just "mimicry on cue." As long as you make this another game, something they and you can have fun doing, it will be absolutely natural to them. And it will enable you to see just how creative your child is.

If your child starts to get bored, change the subject. Come back to it later or another day. The last thing you want to do is take away the "fun" aspect of this whole exercise and make it something the child "has" to do. That's the surest way to ensure that it is the one thing the child will not want to do!

I don't do it any differently when I interview children for the first time in my office, especially small children. First, I try to get them to feel comfortable. I always keep a box with little people, trucks, and cars in my office, for example. I'll let children go through the box before I start "interviewing" them at all. Playing allows them to become very comfortable, and usually puts them in a good mood.

It takes time for a small child to become comfortable with a stranger, to be able to express different emotions "on cue." So once the child is more comfortable with me, I begin by talking about school and their interests. It gives me a very good insight into what's going on in their minds.

Older children are able to express themselves more easily. They just say, "Mom, I want to be on television." "I want to be in commercials." It's not that easy for little children. Yet, as we've seen, the "hottest" age is between four and eight, an age at which most children will *not* know that show business is what they want to do.

But with a little bit of practice—things that you can do with your child at home—it's amazing how wonderful kids can act!

I recently had a five-year-old client come to my office so I could help her prepare for a new ice cream pop commercial audition. She was supposed to make believe that she was sucking on a delicious ice cream pop. We began talking about ice cream—what it felt like when it's in your mouth, how cold it felt, how wonderful it tasted. We practiced in front of a mirror what sucking on an invisible ice cream pop would look and feel like.

Every time the little girl took a lick, she made this wonderful expression with her face, smiling and rolling her eyes, said "uhmmmmm," then took another lick. She wound up getting the commercial. According to the director, she was a natural. Well, maybe, but she was a natural who had *practiced.*

Practice is what it is all about. You just have to work with your child. You have to make it fun. Try a lot of different things. When you're eating dinner, have your child take a spoonful of something he loves into his mouth and say "uhmmmmm, this is great." Then have him try something he hates, and see if he can make a really "yucky" face.

The important thing to remember is that children love to mimic, and children love to do things that are fun. Keep your own acting aspirations for your child to a dull roar—keep it fun—and you'll keep your child motivated.

Now, In The Center Ring...

We need to get your child used to performing in front of people. In one sense, this seems simple—children are always putting on a show. Wanting to be the center of attention is a natural and normal thing for a child.

The important thing is to get the child used to doing it *when it has to be done.* Auditioning is a technique, and rarely do children get more than one chance at auditioning for a particular project. At most auditions, the parents are left in the reception area. The children, one at a time, are taken into another room with a casting director and a video cameraman. They are asked to say the one line or make a particular facial expression to the camera. Rarely will a child get several trys—there simply isn't time to work with the child for any length of time, because there are still thirty or forty children to be seen before the session ends. We're talking about an industry that spends *billions* of dollars on commercials. Time is very important and costly.

Getting your child accustomed to performing when asked is not that difficult. It is, again, a matter of practice. Encourage him to audition for school plays, to volunteer for the color guard in school, to stand up in front of the class and make oral presentations. Work on that with him at home. Make sure he's comfortable.

If he has to stand up in front of a class and read a report, have him do it in front of a mirror. Get him used to watching his facial expressions and practicing how to project the emotion he wants. Most importantly, make sure he practices his "lines"—exactly what he's going to say in his report. I know most parents go over homework with their children, and may very well do all of these things just to ensure their children get good grades. But in this instance, it's also a good exercise to prepare the child for a career in show business.

Does your child like to sing? If he does, do you encourage him to stand up in front of your family and friends and sing for everybody?

When I was a little girl about three years old, I used to love to sing everywhere. When my Mom and I were riding the New York City subways, she always tells me, I would stand up on the seat next to her and start singing. Eventually, everybody sitting in the train would come over to me and listen to me sing.

I don't know if I sang *well,* but she and the other passengers encouraged me. That's probably why I have maintained an interest in this industry. Everybody was always very supportive. Which is why your support is so important.

What If Your Child Is Shy?

Sometimes very shy children like to perform because it gives them an outlet and allows them to express themselves in a way that they normally wouldn't. I find that the shy children who work in this industry are absolutely incredible when they're asked to perform a particular character in a script—it allows them to release emotions that otherwise might be stifled.

Even very famous stars are like that. Carol Burnett frequently talks about how shy she was as a child, and she's fairly shy as an adult. There are a lot of famous movie stars that are extremely shy, yet when they're in a movie or a play, they're absolutely brilliant. So, don't think that if your child is shy he or she may not have the potential to succeed in this business. Many shy children do extremely well.

I've always got my eye out for children wherever I go—at a supermarket, department store, local grocery store, or on public transportation—I'm always observing them. I often wind up sitting next to children, many of them just as shy as your kids. I'll be sitting there, talking to their parents and observing the child from the corner of my eye.

Sometimes I'll start talking about show business. I always like to know how children feel about this particular subject. Nine out of ten times those shy little children light up. They just come to life. Sometimes we'll do little exercises and I'll ask them how they feel about different things. Their parents will immediately say to me, "I can't believe how my child is relating to you, and I can't believe that my child wants to do commercials. My child is usually so shy."

I think you just have to know how to be able to bring this out of a child. As a parent, it's really simple, because nobody knows your child as well as you do. Nobody can motivate your child as well as you can. Whether it's doing well in school or cleaning their room or getting ready for a first audition.

Welcome To Dina's Dance School

Before we discuss the need or importance of lessons, let me make it perfectly clear that I am absolutely *not* telling you to sign your child up for acting lessons, singing lessons, or dancing lessons. I'm *not* looking to have you spend any unnecessary money. From my experience, children who express an interest in taking some sort of classes in the performing arts are very highly motivated children to begin with, and a highly motivated child is one that is likely to be successful.

If your child already takes some sort of lessons, encourage him or her to continue, but always be listening for the signs of boredom or disinterest setting in. I took piano lessons when I was a child. I hated them. But not because I hated the *piano* —I hated the fact that the only music my piano teacher let me play was classical music. Today I love classical music, but I wanted to play contemporary music then. After five years of piano lessons, I quit, although I was very good. I regret it to this day. However, I know that if I my teacher had allowed me to play the type of music that I was interested in at the time, I might well have happily continued my lessons.

Any type of training your child can get in the performing arts is only going to enhance his abilities. The dancing or acting lessons he takes are not necessarily going to help your child only if he becomes an actor. Acting lessons definitely build confidence.

My own children have been taking acting lessons for many years and it has helped them a great deal in school. My oldest daughter's teacher once told me that any time she had to do an oral report, he looked forward to her presentation. She was so enthusiastic. She'd love to get up in front of a class and speak. Not only did she read her report, but she had visual pictures that went along with it. "In fact," he said to me, "She used to put on a show for the class. The class looked forward to every report she did, and so did I." I firmly believe her poise and confidence were directly attributable to her acting classes. And even if she had never acted professionally, they would have obviously helped her in school and life.

You don't have to pay for acting classes. Many YMCAs, YWCAs, YMHAs, YWHAs and a variety of other nonprofit organizations across the country offer wonderful drama classes. Many of them are free, some require a nominal charge. There are always places you can go to get some sort of training if your child wants it. Your local schools probably have school plays that they put on every year, and if your child volunteers for them, even if he just works behind the scenes, he can gain excellent experience.

If your child is interested in show business, how can musical or dance proficiency help him or her? I was recently working on a film and the casting director called me and said they needed a fourteen-year-old boy who could play the drums really well. My daughter had mentioned a boy in her school who was a fabulous drummer. I had recently met his mom in the local supermarket and she said, "You know, all he does is play the drums all day; it's making us crazy. What is he going to do with drums?"

To make a long story short, I sent this young man on the audition and he got the part. You're going to see this kid in a major motion picture—playing Ringo Starr as a child. He's very excited. His mother is thrilled. He's going to wind up making a lot of money and be nationally known. And all because he kept learning the drums *despite* his mother's lack of encouragement.

If you are planning to sign up your child for some sort of lessons, just make sure you keep your priorities straight. Don't sign them up for every class in the world because if you start taking your child on auditions, they're going to miss all those classes.

If your child is not taking any sort of classes at all, ask him how he would feel about taking classes. If he would like to, and you can find something that is free or inexpensive in your area, try it! You have nothing to lose and it will definitely help, but it is not necessary.

One of my biggest clients never took an acting or dancing class in her life and she must have 80 commercials on the air, three major motion pictures under her belt, and was a winner on "Star Search."

So if your children like taking classes, and you can afford them, wonderful. If you can get free classes, even better. If your children never shoot a commercial or make in the business, they will undoubtedly learn something from these classes that will help them in school and later in life.

But it's not the end of the world if they never take a class. And, as the above example makes obvious, it certainly isn't a prerequisite for success!

Chapter 4

Are You Ready For Success?

Let's start with the most important point of all: If you want your child to get involved in show business—to become successful, rich, and famous—you must find the time to devote to your child's career. You can have the most talented child in the world, but if you or someone else is not available to take him to auditions and callbacks, the child should wait until he's old enough to do it on his own. Otherwise, you'll be spinning your wheels...and giving your child's dreams short shrift.

Do You Have The Time?

Yes, it's a huge commitment on your part, and *no one is forcing you to make it*. If you say you will make the commitment, but then are not willing (or are simply unable) to invest *your* time in your children's success—and undergo the initial financial sacrifices I'll discuss later in this chapter—*then don't waste* **their** *time.*

I know it's likely both you and your spouse work, which only makes the time commitment more difficult. But most of my clients have two hard-working parents. A lot of them are not professionals, which means they are tied more tightly to time clocks and have far less leeway to fit an audition in, say, between sales calls. Nothing is different.

If this really is what you and your child want to do, you'll find the time. We all find time to do the things we want and that we feel are important. Just remember: You don't *have* to.

A Day In The Life...

It would probably help if I gave you a better idea of your typical day if you have a child in show business. First of all, you won't necessarily be in it alone. Most likely, your child's manager (like me) will act as liaison with you and the "rest of the business"—agents, casting directors, producers, etc.

It all starts at the manager's level. Agents will call me up, for example, and say, "Tomorrow we're working for McDonald's, and we need children between the ages of seven and nine from all ethnic backgrounds. Would you please give us the names of your clients that fit this category?" After looking through my roster, picking out the clients I feel are suitable, and passing them along, the agent—either later that day or the following day—will call me and give me audition times for each of the clients I suggested.

Now usually there is at least one day's notice—I'll know on Monday who's scheduled for Tuesday and have the rest of the day to confirm the appointments with my clients' parents. But there are certainly occasions when I get early-morning requests for auditions that same afternoon.

If it's during the school year, auditions are set up after school—any time between 3:30 and 6:00 p.m. It's doubtful that more than one or two of my clients, if that, live near the audition site. The majority will have to travel forty-five minutes, an hour, even two hours to the audition.

As a manager, I try to arrange convenient times for my clients, depending on where they live. The further they live from the audition, the later the time I try to get them. Unfortunately, sometimes so many children are being seen for a particular role that I really don't have a choice of times—I have to take the time I'm given.

What does this mean—practically—to my clients and their parents? If there's a 3:30 appointment time, and my client lives an hour from the audition, I *know* the mother has to take the child out of school early to get to the audition promptly. (Being late is simply never a viable option.) Neither I nor the mother are probably thrilled about this circumstance, but that's the nature of the business.

The only way to keep a modicum of control given this reality is to remember that you do have some alternatives. Some of my clients' parents have worked out arrangements with their bosses. If the mother knows there is an audition later that day, she's allowed to skip her lunch hour and leave an hour early to take her child to the audition. Some of the parents are able to work overtime, "saving up" hours so when their children have auditions, they can get the time off by "drawing from their savings."

Once you start going on auditions, you will quickly meet other parents living in your area who are doing the same thing. A lot of parents get together and car pool to the auditions. Sometimes dads work at night, so they are free during the day to take their children on auditions.

Another option you should never lose sight of is that you can simply say "No." Besides being a manager, I'm a mother, and I have certainly seen situations in which the impossible was just that. In such situations you simply have to let the opportunity go by. You don't *have* to go on the audition. It's not life or death. And you certainly don't have to go on *every* audition. If your manager is good, she or he will understand that you occasionally have to pass.

Some of my mothers have such strict schedules and/or live so far from the usual audition sites that we have simply limited the number or type of auditions on which to send their children—narrowly-defined roles, very particular commercials. Other parents have no car and are at the mercy of public transportation. While I try to factor this into any appointment equation, allowing extra time for the vagaries of buses and trains, the lack of a car may well limit your child's availability, too.

Getting your child to an audition should not be a nerve-wracking expedition that leaves you and the child exhausted and angry—not the best condition in which to reach an audition! Nobody expects you to turn your life totally upside down. There's a limit to what any of us can do. We try. We do our best. If you can only take your child on auditions once a week, don't let that discourage you—some of the most successful children in the business miss more auditions than they make. They do not live two minutes from the auditions, and their parents are not free all day.

There Are Sometimes Ties For First

It's also important that you keep your child's career in perspective. If your child likes to act—but also likes the piano, or sports, or simply playing with friends—you don't necessarily have to put him in a position where he has to choose between two things he loves equally. A show business career does not have to be an overwhelming and overbearing one.

I have a client who is extremely successful—he has a recurring role on a soap opera and is featured in a number of commercials. His parents, while happy for his success, have a very healthy attitude about it: They want to make sure their child also gets to enjoy being a kid. Away from the "grease-paint," they want him to lead as normal a life as possible. Which means they keep his career in perspective.

The kid loves his career. But he is also an absolute baseball nut. During his Little League baseball season, his mother gives me a list of every ball game so I can mark those dates on a calendar. If someone wants him to audition during those times, she (and he) will not go, and I don't blame her.

You have to keep everything at a very even keel. Your child's success is based on *your* ability to keep everything running smoothly, to successfully juggle being a spouse, mother, worker, coach, positive role model...Superparent! If you feel that you don't want to audition for a couple of weeks—that *you* need a break—take it. There are projects every day, every week, every month, year after year. If you decide that you don't want to audition or you want to put your child's career on hold for a few weeks, go ahead. The world won't stop, show business will go on. You have to do what you need to do for the welfare of your child and your family, and that is extremely important. *That's* what creates success.

Remember, you don't have to go on ten auditions every day of the week for your child to be successful. A successful child is one who is motivated, supported by family, and guided by a professional.

Stiff Upper Lips Come In Handy

If your child has gone to a few auditions and not gotten the jobs, especially if it's been difficult for you to get him there, you may begin to get discouraged. Always keep in mind that legitimate agents and managers work on commission only. *We don't earn one cent unless your child works,* so there is no reason why we would consistently send your child out on auditions unless we felt your child had the potential to work in the industry. You must believe this!

All my successful clients have parents who hesitated, who really didn't believe that this could happen to their child. *All of them.* Not *one* parent has ever walked into my office and said, "I know my child's going to be a star, and that's it." They all *wanted* their children to become stars and they all knew that it would take work on their part, but few of them believed their dreams were even remotely possible.

But keeping a positive attitude requires more than just desire—everyone has that. The conviction you must cultivate in yourself and in your child is "I can do this; *we* can do this." The children who make it through the inevitable rejection are the ones insulated by parents consistently reinforcing one message: You can do it!

As you start going on auditions and "making the rounds," you'll pretty much see the same people over and over again. One day, you'll go on an audition and a familiar face will be missing. Two or three auditions go by and you still don't see her. A few weeks, a few months, you'll notice other people missing. What happened? They quit! They gave up!

They got discouraged, lost their positive attitudes, and be-came casualties of the business. It happens every day. Many people lose heart and drop out. Only the parents who per-severe and keep trying eventually see their children make it.

Remember: The absolute key to your child's success is *your* commitment to hang in there, even when you don't see immediate results.

If your child has potential, stay with it. Hang in there. Don't let people discourage you. Your child will become suc-cessful. It has happened over and over and over again.

You also must realize that maintaining a positive attitude is encouragement for your child. When your child walks out of an audition, he may think he didn't do well. Just tell him, "Forget it! There's going to be another audition next week. You'll do much better there."

If you know in your heart that your child is going to be successful, then he will be. Just think about all those commercials you've seen on television and how often you've said to yourself, "My child is cuter than that kid. *My* child can do that." You're right. Your child *can.*

Whose Objectivity Is It, Anyway?

Several years ago, a cute little five-year-old girl walked into my office with her mother. She came to me through a recommendation of one of my other clients. She was outgoing, very talkative, and didn't hesitate about talking to strangers—the qualities that I look for. The mother immediately let me know that she didn't believe that her child was anything special. She was there only because the other mother had nagged her to come! In fact her exact words were, "I think my daughter is absolutely wonderful, but I'm her mother, and I'm supposed to say that."

After spending a couple of minutes with her daughter, I knew this little child *was* extremely special, and that she would probably be very successful in show business if she applied herself. I urged the mother to see what I had seen: "Look, you don't even need pictures. You don't have to invest a penny, but give me the opportunity, let me try. Let me send your child on a couple of auditions and let's see how she does."

Her response: "Fine, I'm willing to take her, but I think I'm wasting my time—I don't see how a mother could be objective with her own child."

I explained to her that it really didn't matter if she were objective. All she had to be was positive and encouraging! "If you want your child to be successful in this business," I told her, "Your attitude and the way you relate to your child is really the key."

We started sending the child on auditions. On the first audition the child got a callback. I was very excited. I called up the mother and said to her, "I have great news for you. Your child got a callback."

Again the mother downplayed the whole thing: "Oh, well, probably because she was the cutest kid in the whole room, and maybe they just didn't have a cute bunch of kids show up at this audition." Nevertheless, the child went on the callback.

Three days later the casting director called to tell me that they were very interested in the little girl for this particular project. His only hesitation was that the mother did not want to come back another time! When he had talked to her in the reception area, her response was, "Well, what for? She's not going to get it anyway, and I don't want to waste my time."

The casting director was concerned. If the mother's attitude was so negative, would the child readily respond as expected at the commercial shoot?

I called the mother immediately. "Look," I said, "The casting director called me and he really *would* love to use your child in this particular commercial. Unless *you* convince him not to, your child will probably wind up making $40,000 or $50,000 on this project *this year*. However, he is very worried that because your attitude is so negative, it's going to affect the child's behavior on the set."

The mother remarked, "To be honest with you, it's so hard for me to believe that my child is going to be in a commercial."

"Well, believe it," I answered. "It's happening after *one* audition. But unless you change your attitude, your child is not going to work. Everyone is going to be afraid to use her."

The mother did wind up going back with the child, and her attitude was totally different. The casting director called me and said, "Boy, what did you say to this woman?" Now, I don't know if it was the money that changed her (though I'm sure the amount got her attention), but when the casting director asked the mother if she was available for the particular dates that they would be shooting the commercial, the mother said, "Absolutely, definitely, whatever you want. I'll work it into my schedule."

The little girl wound up booking the commercial, for which she earned $63,000...that year. We just renegotiated the commercial. It's going to run for another year, and she's probably going to double that amount. Talk about a positive attitude! This mother has the most positive attitude you could ever want. She is extremely supportive of her child. I guess that it's just a hard thing to comprehend that your child will be successful, that your child will make lots of money. However, she certainly *can*. And your attitude is vitally important.

Keep Cain & Abel Out Of Your Home

As your child begins to work, the entire family will be faced with sacrifices that will affect all of them. What sacrifices you and your family decide to make are totally within your control. How much effort you put into making your child successful in this business is totally up to you. And you are the one who determines how much of a priority that career is.

Although there is not necessarily a right way, a best way or, for that matter, an obviously *wrong* way to achieve a successful career for your child, I think there are certain steps you can take to balance your family's lifestyle with the requirements of your child's career.

First and foremost, never force this business on your family. (Certainly never force it on your child!) If you do, you will find the strain can rapidly tear apart whatever harmony exists. Rather than being something the entire family can enjoy and in which all of its members can participate, your child's career will become a source of resentment to everyone else. Neither you nor your spouse nor your other children have to give up everything you love in life. None of you need stop living your own lives in order to be at the disposal of your child's career. If you and your family choose to make show business part of your lives, do it according to your schedules and your priorities.

Second, remember that the decision *is* a family one, not just one between you and your child. The entire family gets involved when a child starts a show business career. If you have other children in the family who are not pursuing a career in show business, they may get jealous over all the attention that this particular child is getting.

I am convinced there are ways to work through any such rivalry or jealousy. I definitely do *not* believe that the other children in the family should lose out or be disappointed. They certainly shouldn't have to rearrange their lives around the child who's trying to get in show business. As a parent, you must help everyone feel that they are a part of the one child's success—that every booking, every successful audition, every role is a *team* effort.

You must also help each of your other children identify their particular talents—sports, music, dance, whatever—and give them every opportunity to maximize them. With all your other responsibilities, this may well test your sanity and lead to early exhaustion! Which is why you will quickly become better organized and begin to set limits on what you can and can't do—including how much time you can devote to your child's career.

Another important consideration for your entire family—especially when your child begins scoring success after success—is to make sure your "Donna" doesn't quickly become a *prima donna*. I have clients who are extremely successful, earning more money in one year than you and your husband may earn in your lifetimes. Yet you would never know that these children are earning a penny. They are very down-to-earth—they still have chores to do at home, they still have to keep up their school grades. They're just regular kids...with hefty bank accounts. Their parents and families would simply not tolerate anything else and make sure that the child keeps his or her success in perspective.

Have Your Travel Card Handy

An especially demanding situation arises when a particular commercial or TV or movie role requires travel. If your child becomes successful, some travel is inevitable, so you need to be ready for it. The time will come, for example, when your child will have to be separated from the rest of the family—maybe he's shooting a project in another part of the country. Will you be available to go with this child? Will you be able to make arrangements for the other children in your family? If you're not available to go with your child, is there somebody of legal age who is?

Somebody over eighteen *must* go with your child. Maybe you can't take off from work, or your other children are too young and you don't have anyone to leave them with. Possibly you have a child who is over eighteen and they can go with this child. Maybe there is a grandparent who would like to go. Prepare for this in advance so you are not caught in a mad scramble for a warm chaperone body when the good news comes!

If it does, don't worry about the finances. This business is very high paying and very generous. All expenses will be paid for the child *and* the parent or guardian, and everything will generally be first class—air, hotel, food, etc. You won't have to lay out a penny. Once your child gets the job, everything is taken care of.

But what about before your child gets the job? While you and she are still *schlepping* from audition to audition and class to class?

You Will Spend *Some* Money

I have advised you not to pay a fortune to some charlatan for "professional pictures" and noted that reputable agents and managers require no up-front monies to take on your child as a client. Nevertheless, as you begin your trek down the show biz road, there are, inevitably, some expenses you will have to bear. Just remember that they are always, to a great degree, under your control, since you control the pace of your journey.

Transportation

As you start going out on auditions, be prepared to spend more on gas and public transportation. And the more you audition, the more money you will have to spend to get there. The car pooling idea mentioned earlier is one way to keep these expenses in line.

Telephone

Your phone bills will go up as you place more calls to and spend more time on the phone with agents and managers. Even if the agents and managers are calling you, I can guarantee that most of those calls will be collect. That's the way the business is, at least for someone just coming out of the blocks.

Does this seem unfair to you? As a manager, I receive over one hundred pictures a week from all over the country. After my appearance on *Live with Regis and Kathy Lee,* I received over one *thousand* phone calls and pictures from parents all across the country. Fortunately, most of them included a self-addressed, stamped envelope, so I was able to respond to each and every one of them. However, so many other people sent me pictures (and I know they were very expensive pictures) without envelopes and postage that it was just physically impossible to invest the time (or hire someone) to send back the pictures, let alone pay for the postage myself.

Parents have called me from every state in the Union and, in some instances, kept me on the phone for an hour or more, asking about how their children can get into show business. If I have the time, I don't mind using it to talk to parents. But neither I nor other managers can afford to call them back on our nickels.

It's important to remember that we all work on commission, a percentage of what each client *earns.* When a manager like myself takes on a new child as a client, we begin incurring a lot of expenses, not the least of which are phone calls to agents and casting directors. We mail numerous pictures. We must attempt—at our expense—to remind everyone involved in a project for which your child may be right that your child is out there, that he or she should be auditioned, that he or she has been doing "X" and "Y." Promotion is our business. And we will have invested a significant amount of time and money before your child earns a penny. Before, in other words, *we* earn a penny.

Postage

You will need to pay the postage to mail out pictures to agents and managers who, you hope, will agree to represent your child. While mailing out five pictures won't hurt most budgets, mailing out a hundred or two hundred suddenly starts adding up. But if you wish your child to be represented by a reputable manager, it will be important to send his or her calling card wherever possible.

Dental Expenses

You may need to invest in some dental work for your child —as little as a thorough teeth cleaning and/or "whitening," as much as fixing a discolored tooth, braces, orthodontic work (the latter two for older children) to correct more serious defects. A flipper or bridge may be necessary for younger children with missing teeth.

Haircuts

It's very important that children always be neatly groomed, so you may have to have more frequent haircuts, especially if a spate of auditions are coming up. If you are on a very tight budget, learning how to trim your child's hair to keep it neat between major haircuts may well be advisable.

Clothing

Your clothing costs may go up, especially if you want to purchase an outfit or two strictly for auditioning. But keep one thing in mind before you head for the department store's highest-priced aisles: When children audition for commercials, they should almost *always* dress casually. At this point, producers and casting directors are *not* looking for glamour. They are looking for regular kids, and they want them in regular school or play clothes.

On the other end of the spectrum, avoid any clothing that is tattered or torn. What I suggest is that you buy a neat pair of jeans and a polo shirt (and/or a sweatshirt in the winter time). If you already have clothes that are casual but very neat, you may not need *any*thing new.

Babysitting

If you have other children, you probably won't be able to bring them along to auditions. Casting directors' offices are frequently very tiny, and they just don't have the room for a lot of children. If every mother brought along the child who was auditioning plus the rest of her family, there would be no room for any other children!

Additionally, your other childrens' schedules of school, sports or extracurricular activities may make it impossible to coordinate a whole "family" trip, especially if the audition is on very short notice.

So be prepared to have arrangements ready-made for last-minute babysitting. If your spouse can't fill in, you have no other family members in the area, and you can't find a neighbor willing to "hold down the fort," this may well necessitate paying babysitters. Please factor this cost into your budget.

Stage Mothers Don't Grow Fangs

Just remember: I or any other manager can do my job to perfection, but my impact on your child is insignificant compared to yours. You alone really know what makes Mark tick. How to motivate him. How to encourage him. When to give him a break. When to push a little harder. *You* are the key to his success, and don't ever let anyone tell you differently.

Everyone is going to have advice for you. Don't listen to them. Don't listen to other **mothers**. Don't listen to strangers.

The best advice that I can give you is go by your gut feelings, because 99 percent of the time they will be right.

Do you know what a "stage mother" is? To many of you, it probably conjures up an image of some horrible woman pushing her unwilling child onto a stage to perform in front of a roomful of strangers. That woman has a name, but "mother" isn't part of it.

This is not even close to what a true stage mother needs to be. A stage mother is someone who is supportive, encouraging, and willing to give the child room to grow and develop. She will allow him to have his bad moods as well as his good ones. Her only "pushing" should be to make sure her child stays a regular kid, whatever his or her ultimate success.

A stage mother is, ultimately, one who understands that there is a life *away* from show business.

Also keep in mind that your child is going to get all the attention, and there's not going to be any glory in it for you. It's you *child's* career, no matter how essential you are to it.

Keep Sight Of Your Goal

Remind yourself often that everyone has a bad day, even children. I would suggest that if your child doesn't do his or her best at an audition, forget it! If you make a big deal about it, your child will stop having fun and lousy auditions will quickly become the norm. Maybe your child has been going to a lot of auditions and needs a break. Give it to him. This is not life or death. Just make it fun. Don't let it take over his life or yours.

One of my clients, up for a major role in a motion picture, must have had about four callbacks, until it finally came down to him and one other child. The other child got the role, but because they liked my client so much, they still gave him a small part in the picture.

His mother had the best of perspectives. Her comments to me reflected the attitude you will hopefully have when your child finishes second: "You know, we went on so many call-backs, and after each one, our hopes soared higher. Well, he didn't get that role, but he's so excited, and I couldn't be happier."

This child really didn't care if he got the big role or a little role—he was just happy to be in the movie. Coming in second didn't matter to him, and his mother didn't let it matter to her.

As a result of this incidental role, a major casting director saw the child and decided to cast him as the lead in another project. You can imagine how excited this whole family was. He got the major role after all!

What if this mother had decided that if her child did not get the major role, he wouldn't be in the film? It's happened! Don't let it happen to you. You may think, "My child will be so disappointed if he doesn't get the major role, he's not going to want to take a small role." Such attitudes are learned. You need not be the teacher!

If children took this business too seriously, they would probably be neurotics before the age of twelve. As a manager, I want them to remain kids while they're working professionals. As a parent, you need to want the same thing.

Chapter 5

Education, Rejection, Direction

Three inevitable questions arise as your child starts seriously auditioning and working:

1. What happens when my child has to miss school to audition or work?
2. I know my child is not going to get every job. How do I help her handle the rejection? How do *I* handle it?
3. What can I do to help my child take direction and criticism better?

Grades Are First Priority

Since there really are no guarantees in this business, your child's education should be your top priority. And if your child becomes successful, school is *more*, not less, important.

If it ever becomes necessary for your child to miss a day of school, he must be able to pick up his classwork and homework assignments quickly and easily. School should not be made more difficult for your child because he now has an acting career. And the better he does in school, the more likely he will be able to gain the cooperation of his teachers.

There are things you can do to help your child. Speak to his teachers. Make sure they understand that he will be going on auditions and that getting homework assignments early will make it easier for him to juggle school and a career. There's a lot you can do to integrate a show business career into your child's school life, but you've got to get the cooperation of the teachers and the principal. As long as your child's grades are kept up and he does well in school, there should be absolutely no problem with either.

Most of my mothers are very strict about having their children do their homework during audition trips. Many times, if the children work on a feature film, there is a tutor that is supplied and the children don't miss any school at all—they get virtually individual attention on the set. But tutors are not always available, so it's important that you work with your child to keep up his grades. Do what you have to do to make sure he does well.

Sometimes children fall behind and are told they can't go on auditions until they pick up their grades. Their grades improve so fast you wouldn't believe it! The children that are successful do very well in school—they have to.

Acting can even make a student better. Several years ago I represented a young boy whom I recommended take some local acting classes. I didn't realize he had a learning disability—I just thought he needed help in putting expression into his reading. He was bright, good looking, and had a tremendous desire to succeed. I felt that just a couple of classes would help his copy reading improve. (When reading a script, the flow of words has to be very natural, not in a monotone. It has to flow with expression.)

After about four sessions in his acting class, his teacher from school called me and said, "What happened to him? His reading skills have increased so much. There's a new child in my class." I told her that this was because he had taken acting classes and, aside from his confidence in his reading being increased, he had learned techniques to improve his reading. The teacher was impressed, the mother was ecstatic. This boy booked three or four commercials very quickly.

Tennis Commercial, Anyone?

Most interviews for children during the school year are set up after school hours. However, during the summer months, they are scheduled at any time. (Note: Auditions for babies and young adults are scheduled all day throughout the year.) If your child has filled up after school time with clubs or sports or classes, make sure he's not going to be upset if he misses them.

Many children—including many working actors—love sports and play sports at school. Sports teach many useful lessons, too, plus they're fun. So if your child really wants to be involved with a particular team, I certainly wouldn't categorically dissuade him. But he probably will need to deal with the possibility of missing an occasional practice. This might necessitate you or your spouse talking to his coach, explaining the way auditions are scheduled, and getting his permission for your son or daughter to miss an occasional practice.

There are other good reasons to not only allow your child's participation in sports, but to encourage it. I get a tremendous number of calls involving commercials where they need a kid who plays tennis or baseball or soccer. I've even gotten calls for entire teams!

That's right. Sports is the common denominator in a lot of children's commercials. There was a McDonald's commercial on the air that ran for a very long time. It opens up with a little girl in a ponytail hitting a ball with a bat. That was one of my clients. This little girl was on a Little League team, loved it, and here it paid off. Her mother used to say to me, "Ah, she's got practice this afternoon. She can't do that audition." And I used to say, "Fine, let her do what she likes to do. It's important. It's going to help her." And it did. She got paid for doing the *other* thing she liked most!

Show business is highly competitive, so children involved in competitive sports have a great edge—they learn to handle rejection, a major part of this business.

Speaking Of Rejection

We all know what happens if we promise our children something, and, for whatever reasons, can't deliver. We know how to present the news to our child so she will not be extremely disappointed. If we have promised to take our child to an amusement park and wake up feeling sick, or it's raining, we don't tell her, "Guess what, we're not going, hah hah, too bad," because we know that's really going to upset her. She may be disappointed, but she shouldn't have to be devastated!

In this business, 99 percent of what your child will see is rejection. Every day could well be raining and cancel that amusement park trip! So learning how to help your child cope with a fact of life—and learning how to cope yourself—is not just important, it's essential.

No one will call and tell you your child didn't get a role. You will be notified only if the child gets a part. So he can audition for ten projects and no one's going to call you up and say, "Well, he didn't get #1, #2, or #3...." It doesn't work that way. You only get feedback on the job you get.

Keep this in perspective. Just because your child auditioned for a role and didn't get it doesn't mean he didn't do well. It doesn't even mean he wasn't absolutely perfect for the part! The producers may have cancelled the entire project; they may have switched the role from a boy to a girl; they may have changed the age range. There are a million reasons why your child did not get the role. Remember, he would not be auditioning unless he was prepared to audition, and the fact that he's auditioning is positive. Not every child can walk into a room with a stranger and perform on cue.

There can be anywhere from 30-400 children auditioning for every role. When your child's confidence level is at its highest, he's going to walk out of every audition and say, "Mom, I know I got it." Even if he doesn't get the part, he will know that he did his best and that the reason he didn't get the role had absolutely nothing to do with his acting ability. It was either that he was too short, too tall, too fat, too thin, too dark, or too pale. There was something he had no control over.

As I have said before, auditioning has to be fun, and if it is fun, then the child who experiences rejection will not take it to heart. You, as his supportive parents, should make sure that he considers it nothing more than an experience to be enjoyed. I look at rejection as a positive. Every audition gives the child a bit more experience. He may learn something he can use later. It is part of the ladder to success.

Some children take rejection naturally. When they lose a role, they don't have a second thought about it. They audition, they come home, they forget about it. Life goes on. They'll audition for something else.

Who's Been Rejected?

It's probably the minority of children who need you around to buck up their confidence Frankly, the question I hear most frequently doesn't come from my clients, but from their parents: "How I can handle the rejection of my child?"

Parents get discouraged long before the children do. Children who succeed in this business, who *want* to do this, find auditioning and meeting agents, managers, and casting directors a fun thing to do. They learn to take rejection in stride ...sooner or later.

Parents generally make more of the rejection than the kids and let it affect them more. Be careful! You must keep your perspective—it's important for your child. If you keep this fun, if you keep it light, then your child is *not* going to be traumatized by the fact that he auditioned for something and didn't get it. All my successful clients experience rejection and they handle it very well. If you were to ask any of the children I represent, "How do you feel when you don't get the job?" they'd all say, "Well, that's part of the business. You can't let it get you down. I'm still enjoying my auditions."

That's how you have to present it to your child. Auditioning is fun, it's a game. If you get a job out of it, well, that's the added benefit. That's how *you* need to look at it, too.

But it's not easy, I'll grant you. Even my most "experienced" mothers are very anxious when their children are up for a major role in a project. And that's only natural. I have several hats. When I'm wearing my "manager hat," I can look at everything very objectively and pooh-pooh nervous parents. But when I take my own children on auditions and wear my "mother hat," I experience the same feelings of anticipation before the audition, the same feelings of disappointment if my child doesn't get the role. Yet I know that it's *me* feeling the rejection, that it's *me* harboring the disappointment, not my children. And I just remind myself to not let my feelings influence them.

But don't think it isn't a hard thing to do. How would you feel if, after several auditions, the choice for a major role was between your child and another, and the other child got the role? Would you find that encouraging or discouraging? What if it consistently happened? Would you feel you were getting closer, or that she'd never get anything?

You have to look at it positively—your child came very close to being chosen. She's good and improving. That's the encouraging thing. If this consistently happened, and if your child frequently got a callback, I would say that was wonderful, couldn't be better. Because it means that your child has all the qualifications for that particular role. What happened was that the other child was just a little taller, a little shorter, a little fatter, a little thinner—a little different physically than your child. And the director liked the other "look." Who knows what the real reason was? The fact that she got very close to it—*that* is the encouraging sign you need to look for.

You may have a long time to practice your response to rejection. I represent a little girl who went on *85* auditions over several months before she booked her first role. Fortunately, she had a very positive-minded mom and she hung in there. This mother never gave up, and this child is today one of the top bookers in the business—with more than 60 commercials under her belt. (Landing a role is called a "booking." Children that book a lot of jobs are called "big bookers.")

Helping Your Child Work

Your work doesn't end when your child finally lands a job. Sometimes it takes eight hours to shoot the 30-second commercial you see on television. A child could be asked to say the same thing a hundred times. It's not necessarily because he's not doing it right, but simply because the director wanted to try several different approaches. There could also be technical problems—the lighting angle's not right, the camera angle's off, the camera breaks down.

For whatever reason, it is not unusual for a child shooting a commercial to have to say the same line with the same genuine emotion ten, twenty or one hundred times. Or to try it slightly differently once, twice, ten times. Will your child be able to do it?

Your answer to that question is the answer the casting director would like to know. Because it costs lots of money to do a commercial, and the producer and the sponsor need to know that your child will take direction, which means doing what they say—when they say it—without fighting back.

Asking your child some questions may give you a pretty good insight into his personality. When he's doing something, does he feel that his way is always better than someone else's? Even if his way is excellent, could he put his feelings aside and still try to use someone else's suggestion? That's important. You should discuss this with your child.

For example: Grab one of his toys that has interlocking pieces. Put it in front of him and ask him to put it together for you. Then, instead of putting piece number one in a certain place, ask him to substitute piece number three, even if it doesn't fit. See how he reacts to your suggestion.

That's what doing commercials is all about. He could be asked to say, "Wow, this tastes great" for a product that he hates. But, if he says, "Wow, this tastes great" convincingly, he's going to wind up making a lot of money. I would say children who do commercials usually average about $10,000 for each commercial, and some of my clients have 70 commercials on the air.

If you can explain to your child that when he auditions or is on a shoot, and he's asked to say something differently or repeatedly, that it's just make-believe and part of the job, you will have taken another important step to getting your child ready for success.

Section Two

Camera!

Getting The Word Out

Chapter 6

Creating
Your Calling Cards

I know you're ready—I know you're anxious. You don't want to hear anything else about positive attitudes. Your attitude couldn't *be* any more positive. You have made arrangements for your other children to be taken care of while you take your child on auditions. You have taken care of time off with your boss. You're ready to go. You want your child in show business. You want your child making a lot of money. You don't want more talk. You want to know what to do.

The Importance Of Pictures

This is the first real step you're going to take on the road to show business—getting pictures of your child.

Wait a minute! Don't get nervous. I'm *not* sending you to a professional photographer. This is *not* going to cost you a lot of

money. I'm going to show *you* how to take the pictures you'll
need. The only required equipment is a 35 mm camera and
some black & white film.

Before we start snapping away, let's clear up some of the
terms used in this business. First of all, no one says "picture."
They say "head shot." Head shots are 8 x 10, black and white
photographs of someone from the shoulders up.

Head shots are one of the most important tools you will
ever need in this business, because they are your calling
cards! They are probably the best way of getting your foot in
the door of a manager, agent, casting director or producer's
office. Head shots are where the casting process starts.

When a writer creates a script, he mentally visualizes
what each character in his story will look and sound like. It is
then that the casting director's job begins. She goes through
her file of head shots to determine whom she will call to audition based on their physical resemblance to the character in
the script.

This is why it is absolutely essential that a head shot actually look like your child. Head shots focus the casting director's attention, but nothing is worse than a casting director
who expects one person to walk through the door and suddenly sees another! Make sure your head shots make your child
look the same as he will when *he* walks through the door.

I need to roll off on a tangent here. Projects (commercials,
TV shows, soaps, movies, etc.) in show business are broken
down into two categories: commercials and "legit," the latter
being anything *other* than a commercial—including television series, soap operas, pilots, situation comedies, major
motion pictures, made-for-television movies, Broadway, off-
Broadway, community theater, industrial shows, etc.

I gave you an example earlier of how I get a commercial
breakdown from an agent—what is involved in the shoot,
what children they are going to need, what age ranges.

Head shots are really not necessary for commercials because casting directors give appointments out to agents based on the names that they are given, not the pictures. Very rarely are commercials very explicit concerning exact requirements. They may say "We want redheads for this commercial" or "We only want black children," but otherwise, a wide of variety of "looks" might be appropriate.

Breakdowns for legit roles are more specific. When an agent is working on a legit project, he will call me and say, for example, "I'm working on a remake of *Huckleberry Finn*, and I'm looking to cast the role of Huck." Now we all know that Huck Finn was a little boy about ten years old, with blond hair, a cowlick, and a couple of freckles on his turned-up nose. The casting director will expect pictures of children who fit the role physically—no dark-haired boys, no redheads, no eight-year-olds, no twelve-year-olds, and, obviously, no girls!

That's why it's important to have a good picture of your child, a true representation of what your child looks like. The last thing you want is for your child to walk into an audition and have the casting director say, "I want to see the child who looks like this picture, not the one that just walked in."

Shooting Your Own Head Shots

You're already so experienced taking pictures of your child anyway, you'll find taking "professional-looking" head shots very easy. Here's how to get started:

1. Let your child know ahead of time why you're doing this and when you're planning your "shoot"—I want him or her to be very enthusiastic and excited about this.

2. Decide where you're going to take the pictures. Walk through your house, room by room. Have you come across a wall that is solid colored? We want to keep away from a busy background—it will just detract from the child's face.

Is the room brightly lit? If not, brighten it up—bring in a couple of extra lamps, put a couple of heavy wattage bulbs in the fixtures.

If you can't find an appropriate plain wall, just tack up a sheet—white or pale gray, blue or yellow—and create your own photographer's backdrop.

3. Place a stool or chair in front of the sheet or plain wall.

4. If you have unsteady hands, attach the camera to a tripod—a three-legged apparatus that the camera rests on so you don't have to hold it. But you don't need to run out and buy a tripod. You can place your camera on a high shelf or even on another chair piled with books so you can get behind it. This way you don't have to hold the camera and it will be steady. There is a lot we can do to improvise.

Getting Your Child Ready

I've already stressed the importance of these shots being "realistic." So be very careful. Don't dress up your daughters. Don't put lots of makeup on them. Don't dress your sons in suits. Your children have to look like they look every day when they go to school.

I want your child to look like a regular kid in the pictures, so dress him or her in casual clothing, preferably in solid colors, which won't detract from his or her face. I would prefer that you didn't use black or white, because sometimes the contrast is too harsh. But if that's all you have, well, don't go out and buy any clothing for your child. Use what you have.

I always like a plain collar. A simple oxford shirt with a little collar and a crew neck sweater is probably your best choice. I don't want him in a V-neck sweater without a shirt because it tends to look sloppy, and I don't like turtlenecks on children because I've never seen anyone in a turtleneck that looked relaxed.

If you don't have a crew neck sweater, a round-necked sweatshirt is fine. Have the collar tucked in. It presents a nice clean-cut collegiate look. Nothing fancy.

Girls should avoid wearing earrings or anything in their hair—barrettes, ribbons, etc.—because they tend to distract from the face. Hair, obviously, should be clean and shiny, and styled in a manner appropriate to your child's age.

If your child is considering a new haircut, *this is the time to get it.* If they want to change their hair style, have them do it now, because you want them to look like their pictures.

Again, avoid heavy makeup of any kind. Children should look like children, not gussied-up tiny adults. If your child has little blemishes or beauty marks and you want to cover them up, use a very light base. Allergies may give some children dark circles under their eyes. These can be lightened slightly. If you want to put on a little clear lip gloss, that's fine. But that's about it.

If your child wears glasses all the time, take the pictures with glasses. If your child only needs glasses for reading, consider omitting them for the picture.

Don't Worry About Poses

When your child is ready, have him or her sit on the stool. Get behind the camera and move it until the child—from the waist up—is centered in the frame.

Explain to your child how to look into the camera lens. It's very important when you look at a head shot to feel that the child is looking directly at you. The child should look directly at the lens.

You don't have to start taking pictures right away. Make sure your child is very comfortable—Talk to him. Make him giggle. Talk about something silly. Tell him he has pudding coming down his face. Have a good time.

Don't pose him—he just has to look into the lens and smile. Maybe saying "cheese" or "jello" will help. As he grins and giggles, start snapping away. You may want to take several roles of film, though I don't think you need to.

Professional photographers take all different types of pictures, but I just want to get you started so you can get your child into an agent's office or a manager's office for representation. Believe me, a regular head shot is all that is needed. Everybody in the world is going to have a comment on what kind of pictures are needed. You're going to hear all kinds of advice. It's going to make your head spin. Ignore it.

Using A Professional Photographer

Some of you may still be nervous about shooting your own head shots and insist on using a professional photographer. If I still can't convince you to do it yourself, let me tell you what to look for and look *out* for when choosing a professional.

(Just keep in mind that professional head shots are *definitely* not necessary for children younger than five. Snapshots are perfectly acceptable. Children under five tend to change so often and so quickly that by the time pictures are shot and developed, the child could look completely different. Save your money.)

Photographers specialize in different subjects. Some shoot landscapes and natural scenes, some shoot products for advertisements, some shoot food, some do portraits. You need to find a photographer who specializes in *children* and who seems to have a great rapport with them.

Do *not* choose a photographer without seeing his work first. Make sure that the pictures you see are of children— *great* pictures of children smiling and in natural poses.

If you're having trouble finding a photographer, you may want to contact the TV and radio stations in your local area—

find out who takes the head shots of their local talent. You can also call local ad agencies or the local photographers association for suggestions. Call several photographers and compare prices, which may range from $50 to $600 for the sitting, plus a contact sheet or proofs.

Proofs And Reproductions

I've contacted several companies on the East Coast, told them that I was putting together a book showing parents how they can get their children into show business legitimately and inexpensively, and asked for their very best prices for developing film, producing contact sheets and bulk quantities of single shots. I think the deal that I have worked out with one of these companies offers the cheapest price you're going to find for reproducing pictures. By no means am I suggesting that you use my reproduction company, but you may want to use their prices for comparison's sake. At the end of this chapter, I have included their name, address, and their price list for the various services we will now discuss.

When you develop your own snapshots, you probably just hand the roll of film to a photo lab or send it to Kodak and specify the type and size prints you want. Professional (and good amateur) photographers take an interim step—looking at a contact sheet.

A contact sheet is an 8 x 10 sheet that reproduces small black & white pictures of the entire roll of film. This makes it much easier (and cheaper) to select the picture you may want to blow up and reproduce. All you might need is a magnifying glass.

Once you have selected the print you want to blow up and reproduce, you again have a couple of options. Reproducing pictures in the "conventional" manner could cost you $250 or more for one hundred 8 x 10's, since it involves enlarging, by hand, each copy from a small negative, which is very time consuming and expensive.

In this industry, "contact print" is the term that is used for reproductions. In this process, the lab simply makes an 8 x 10 negative of the picture you want and runs off as many copies as you need. The process is quick and inexpensive. The best part about it is that you cannot tell the difference between a contact print and a photograph. Shop around. Ask photographers what they would charge you to blow up one hundred 8 x 10's, and you'll see. The prices are astronomical.

When you have selected a pose from the contact sheet, have your photographer make one 8 x 10 blow up of it. You will be charged a "setup charge" for this one blow up—a price that you only have to pay once. Any time you want to reproduce your head shots again, there is no further setup charge. You just pay for whatever number of glossy 8 x 10's you wish.

If you are handling your own reproductions, make sure your child's name appears somewhere on the front of the photograph, preferably along the bottom. I got "my" lab to give me a deal on head shots along with mailing envelopes, which you're also going to need. So ask about them.

Remember: I want you to shop around. I don't want you to feel that you have to use this company. I tried to find a firm that will give you excellent quality work at an extremely reasonable price, but you are free to use any company you choose.

Creating Your Child's Resume

Imagine a casting director trying to match up head shots to the characters in a script. She thinks your child has the face of the little boy in the script. How does she get in touch with you? How does she know how old your child is? What his weight and height are? If he can sing or dance? If he has any experience or training?

She reads his resume—a piece of paper with the child's vital statistics, experience and training pasted to the back of the head shot.

It's very important that a resume be printed neatly and accurately. Anyone looking at a resume should be able to pick out the information at a glance. Your child's name and phone number should be at the top. (By the way, **never put your home address on the resume.** Pictures and resumes are mailed all over the country, and you never know where your head shot may wind up.)

Your child's resume should be divided into four categories:

1. *Vital Statistics:* Height, weight, hair color, eye color; size of shirt or blouse, pants or slacks, dress or suit, shoes; your child's Social Security number. (This is a perfect time to apply for a Social Security number for your child if you haven't done so already. It generally takes about 6-8 weeks to get one after you apply, and without it your child cannot be paid.)

2. *Experience:* A list of your child's "credits"—the amateur and professional work he has done. It could be school plays, dance recitals, community theater, whatever. Include anything you feel represents your child's performing experience.

3. *Training:* List the classes or other training your child has had. Make sure you are brief, listing each individual skill and the years he has been studying it.

4. *Special Skills and Abilities:* The key is to make sure your child stands out from all the rest. Unusual skills are a plus. For example—ear wiggling, skate-boarding, martial arts, etc.

Since regular typing paper measures 8 1/2 x 11 and a head shot is 8 x 10, make sure than when you type or print your child's resume you cut it down so it does not overlap the

picture. I always recommend a few tiny dabs of a glue stick—
if the resume has to be updated it can easily be removed. Keep
it very brief. Don't go into a whole explanation. It isn't necessary.

See the following page for a sample of a winning resume.

Here's the lab I suggest you contact and the prices they
charge for the various services we discussed in this chapter:

Entertaining Ideas, Ltd.
2779 Essex Court
Oceanside, NY 11572

Developing one roll of black & white film and making a contact sheet	$9.95[1]
One-time set-up charge (one 8 x 10 negative make from original print), including art work to place child's name on head shot	$17.50
50 8 x 10 glossy photographs with name printed on front, including cardboard and mailing envelopes	$78.65[2]
100 8 x 10 glossies (as above)	$91.25[2]
100 picture postcards (with child's name and phone number printed on them)*	$64.85[2]
200 picture postcards (as above)	$75.85[2]

* These are discussed in more detail in chapter 8

1 Plus $3.00 postage & handling

2 Plus $10.00 postage & handling

Sample Resume

JOHN DOE

REPRESENTED BY: Name of agent or manager   OR
YOUR PHONE NUMBER (include area code)

PERSONAL:

> Height: 53"
> Weight: 63 lbs.
> Eyes: Blue
> Hair: Blond
> SS#: 123-45-6789
> Birthdate: (Optional)

EXPERIENCE:

> Brown's Elementary School Peter Pan. . . . . . .Lost Boy

SPECIAL SKILLS & TALENTS:

> Singing
> Dance—Tap (4 years)
> Drums—(1 year)
> Little League
> Bike Riding
> Skateboard

TRAINING:

> Cindy's Dance School—Tap

Chapter
7

The Professionals You'll Work With

The whole reason you've spent time taking head shots and money getting them reproduced is to make people in the industry aware of your child, whether for a particular role or to land initial representation.

We've talked about managers and agents and casting directors throughout the book. It's time to give you a more detailed understanding of the role each will play in your child's future.

Personal Managers

Personal managers are your guides to the industry. In general, a personal manager takes a personal interest in representing and grooming your child and making sure that he or she is absolutely ready to start working in the industry.

"Fine" Is Not Fine

Managers prepare your child for interviews and auditions. This is a simple statement, but it encompasses a great deal.

I love finding a child whom I feel has potential in this business and actually preparing that child for a career in show business. I often interview children who aren't really ready to audition, and not because they are untalented. Basically it's because they just don't know what is expected of them. That's where the managers' first function comes in.

The children I represent know exactly how to handle themselves at an interview, whether it's with an agent, a casting director, a producer, or a sponsor. It's the manager's function to make sure they learn exactly how to do that.

Let me give you an example of a typical conversation that may occur between one of these people and my clients. If somebody asked your child, "Hi, how are you?" and your child responded, "Fine," you'd think there was nothing wrong. It's a perfectly reasonable answer to the question...in the world outside show business.

But it is the *wrong* way to begin a conversation with somebody in a position to cast your child in a project. One-word answers to *any* question are to be avoided. If asked, "Hi, how are you?" a professional child might say, "I'm terrific today, and how are you? I feel great. Yesterday I fell and hurt my knee. But it's better now."

The exact content of the answer isn't of primary importance. But the length of the answer is—because the people in *this* business who are interviewing children want to see how verbal the children are, how outgoing they are. And one-word answers don't do that...at least not in a positive way!

A manager will work long and hard on your child's answers to the types of questions that most often come up, long before that child ever goes off to audition. For example, a director may say to your child, "So, you want to be on television. Why do you think you'd like to be on television?" In my office, a child might well say, "Because my Mom wants me to." That's a pretty good reason, but that definitely isn't an answer that I would let one of my clients give to a producer. We certainly don't want to give the casting director or the agent the impression that this child is being forced.

There are a lot of better reasons that a child may give: "I want to make a lot of money." "I want to be famous." "I want to buy toys." "I just think it would be fun." They're all okay. "I don't know" is *not* okay. We want to present our children as extremely outgoing and verbal. Practice this with them. I always suggest, as I did in the past, to do this in front of a mirror. Children get a kick out of seeing their facial expressions in a mirror.

When To Dress Like A Doll

Along with such verbal cues, managers teach children how to handle other aspects of a first interview with an agent or a casting director. They show children how to walk into a room. It's very impressive when a child walks into a room with his hand extended and shakes the hand of the casting director or the agent.

Managers also advise their clients on how they should dress for interviews and auditions. For example, if they want children who are on baseball teams for a particular commercial, I will suggest that any clients I send wear a T-shirt, or, even better, a baseball uniform (if they have one).

I may have gotten a call about a particular doll commercial. Because I know the product, I'll know that the doll that they're using is very glamorous and they want the little girls to actually resemble the doll. I will have my clients go in with their hair in curls, wearing pretty dresses, not as casually dressed as I would normally send them off.

I work with my clients on makeup and hair styles. It a child walks into my office overly made-up, I will explain to them why they shouldn't put themselves in a position of losing a job just because of makeup—I will tell them how much makeup they should wear. If their hair is really teased out, wild looking, or wildly colored, I will tell them that this is going to hold them back. First impressions are lasting impressions.

Making Cold Readings Hot

Another function of being a personal manager is working on copy with children. ("Copy" means lines or sentences in a script.) Sometimes your child will be given "cold copy" to read—meaning that he is given something to read without an opportunity to look it over beforehand.

I always give my potential clients cold copy to read. It gives me an excellent indication of how well they can read and put expression into a script, even without having had a chance to work on it.

When your child auditions, especially for a commercial, the reading is often cold. While your child obviously can't practice something she doesn't have, I can teach her the techniques that will help her address any cold reading in the right frame of mind. We start off practicing "one-liners" in my office, something like, "Wow, this is delicious." There may be suggestions that I can give as to how much expression to give, especially if the child is giving too much or too little. If I feel that the child needs some work in putting expression into what he says, I'll help him. I will have the child come back to my office several times (at no cost to the parents). To me, that is one of the most satisfying parts of my job.

I also spend a great deal of time with the parents, teaching them how to work on copy with their child. A parent is not always available to run into my office with his child so we can work on the script. There are times when it is impossible for me to work on copy with children, so the parents have to be able to coach them.

It's Time To Be Pushy

Once I've gotten the parents and the child to a point where I feel they are ready to meet agents and casting directors—to actually begin auditioning—I will start sending their pictures out. If they haven't already done so, I will help the parents select—from their contact sheet or proofs—the head shot that I feel shows the child off in the best light. Sometimes parents are a little subjective. As a personal manager I know what poses and expressions on the child's face are going to make that child stand out from all the others. Sometimes parents will say to me, "Oh, I don't like that picture. Bennie doesn't really look that good." Nine out of ten times it's the picture that I select that totally flips out all the casting directors.

It's also the personal manager's job to promote your child —to keep everyone in the industry up-to-date on what your child is doing and how he is progressing. Many times I'll send a new client to an agent and his response is, "Well, she's really adorable and she handles copy very well, but I'm a little nervous. I think she's a little bit too new. Why don't you keep us up-to-date on what she's doing and then we'll start sending her out." That's what I do. I make sure everyone knows what my clients are doing—what type of response they've gotten from other agents and casting directors, if they are getting callbacks, if they've started working. I continually send out letters and pictures, talk on the phone, and keep pushing, and pushing, and pushing.

Handholding 101

Probably the most important function of a personal manager is to offer support and encouragement to the parent and the child, especially if they have been going out on auditions for an unusually long time without any results. In one sense, as long as your manager is continuing to send your child out on interviews, you should feel confident—managers only make money if *you* make money; there's really no reason in the world a manager would send your child on interviews *unless that child were employable.*

Statistically it takes a good nine months to a year for a child to start working regularly in the business—to start making money. I'm not going to paint a rosy picture. It's hard work. But you know what? Don't let that discourage you. When my clients are ready to audition, they start booking. I make sure that my clients are totally prepared. They can handle copy and they can handle themselves. However, it *can* get discouraging. I spend a great deal of time on the phone with my clients and their parents, just encouraging them to hang in there.

Sometimes that encouragement works wonders. A mother brought a little boy to my office a couple of years ago. I don't really think he had that much interest in the industry. He was very young, perhaps four years old, so I gave his mother the same advice that I gave you in the beginning of the book. The child was just adorable and I felt that he could be successful, but he needed a little motivation.

About six months passed and the mother came back to me. I took a look at this little boy and my first reaction was, "Wow, has *he* come a long way." The mother did an excellent job. The first audition the little boy went on was for a major role on a new television series—interviews were being carried on simultaneously on both coasts. He was New York's first choice. At the last minute, they decided to use a little boy from L.A., solely because the series was being shot in L.A. and the boy lived around the corner from the studio! Otherwise, it was a toss up between the winner and my first-time auditioner.

You can imagine how excited this little boy and his mother were at getting so close to success the first time out of the blocks. The next two projects that the little boy auditioned for also resulted in callbacks; he wound up coming in second twice more. Within three months, he finally landed a major role. And he's been working ever since.

All the mother had to do was motivate her child. I could have sent this child on interviews six months earlier, but the only thing I would have accomplished would have been to squash any possible interest that the child may have had. You cannot push your child into this business. You can only try to motivate him.

Shooting Big Bird

It's very important that I spend time with my clients, especially the little ones, because children take things so literally. I'm sure many roles have been lost because of a child's baseless but unspoken fears.

Let me give you two funny examples. Not long ago, a five-year-old girl was sitting in my office. We were talking about *Sesame Street* and other favorite shows. Her mother had told me that she mimicked all the commercials, and she knew all the jingles. She was adorable, outgoing, verbal. Everything pointed to success.

The child wanted to do movies but not television. Her mother couldn't figure out why she was such a critic at such a tender age! I finally just asked the little girl, "Wouldn't you like to be on television? Wouldn't you like to appear on *Sesame Street?*"

"I guess I really do want to be on television," she an-swered, And I really want to meet Big Bird. But I'm afraid to be squashed into that box," pointing to the television!

She really thought that people on television had to fit in-side the screen!

My older daughter worked on *Sesame Street* for a number of years, starting at the age of three. My younger daughter almost lived on the set of *Sesame Street* since she always accompanied me when I took her big sister there. Finally, the casting director came over to me and said, "How would you like your younger one to start appearing on the show?'" I was thrilled.

The first scene she had was with Barkley the Dog. They had gone through a couple of rehearsals and then they were ready to shoot the scene. I told my daughter, "Okay, it's time to go on the set because they're ready to shoot you." She looked at me wide-eyed and asked, "Mom, is it going to hurt?"

She thought they were going take a gun and shoot her! Needless to say, once I explained a little "industry jargon," she was fine. And she appeared on quite a number of epi-sodes.

You'll need to work with your children on this "literal" part of their lives. Ask your child if he has any fears. It may be the one thing holding him back.

Agents

My business would not be in existence if it weren't for agents, since most of the auditions I get for my clients come from them.

Agents are licensed by individual states as employment agencies. They are also franchised by the unions—the Screen Actors Guild (S.A.G.), American Federation of Television and Radio Artists (A.F.T.R.A.), and Actors Equity Association

(A.E.A.). It is greatly to my (and your) benefit to work with an agent who is franchised by the major unions. These unions have very strict rules regarding contracts, payments, work hours, etc.

Making Sure You Get Paid

Agents monitor payments. If you have commercials running on the air, you have to be paid every time they air. The union makes sure that this is closely monitored and that you *are* paid. If something happens and you are not paid by a producer, the agent, through the union, will go after the money for you.

Generally, it is the agent's responsibility to submit actors to casting directors and producers. When an agent calls and asks me to recommend clients for a particular project, she in turn will call the casting director and say, "I feel that you should see this child. Please give this child an appointment because he is really right for the role." In other words, the agents are my pushers.

Why do they push my clients? When I call an agent and tell him a particular child is absolutely perfect, the agent knows that my clients are always prepared to audition and that I have never sent a client on an audition when he or she was not right for the role. The agent can confidently push my client to the casting directors.

Sign On The Dotted Line, Please

It is also up to the agent, because he is franchised by the unions to negotiate contracts that conform to their own strict regulations. It is the agent who negotiates the contracts for every project that the child books. Every time you book a project, there is a separate contract.

Commercial contracts are basically the same. They pay $366.50 for an 8-hour shoot. If you run over eight hours, there is overtime. Residuals vary according to the category in which the commercial falls. If a commercial is run during network prime time (meaning that it will air across the country on NBC, ABC, and CBS between 8:00 p.m.. and 11:00 p.m.), it earns the highest fees—your child will receive about $75.00 every time that commercial airs.

That doesn't sound like a lot of money? These commercials can run a lot of times! Some of my clients earn $3,000-$4,000 a week *from a single commercial.*

There are other categories for commercials, and payments will vary with each. Sometimes commercials run, not in every city across the country, but in several small cities and only one or two of the major cities. If they run in the major cities, you get about $50 every time the commercial airs; but if they're confined to smaller cities, the payment is about $25.

Commercials usually run for a year. If a sponsor wishes to have the commercial run another year, then it is the agent's job to renegotiate that contract at a higher fee. Some of my clients have commercials that have been running for five years. I represent a child who booked a commercial for a tiny toy store in a small city six years ago. It was a local commercial, and it only ran during Christmas for two weeks. During the two weeks that this commercial ran, the child earned about $500. The second year, we renegotiated for $1,000. It went to the third year and the child made $1,500. And up every year thereafter.

Now, keep in mind, the child did all her work—one day— six years ago. But she's been earning money every year...and *more* every year. If it is renegotiated next year, she'll earn even more.

If you work on a film, that salary is negotiated by the agent. Naturally, if the child has a lot of experience, he or she could earn as much as $10,000 a week on a film, and the shoot could last from six to ten weeks. But even the minimum to work on a film is $1,500 a week.

No, You *Won't* Work For Free

As I've stressed before, agents and managers work on commission, and they only get paid when your child works.

For those of you who worry about such fees, don't. As I've reminded more than one parent, the more money you're paying out in commissions, the more money you're *earning*.

I've had parents come to me and say, "We'll work for free. I just want my child to work, that's all we care about." I don't believe that *any*one should work for free. *My* clients certainly don't. I make sure that my clients are paid top money. I have confidence that the agents I deal with will negotiate the best contracts.

Yes, it sounds exciting and wonderful to have your child "in the business." I know how you feel. You just want to see your child in a commercial.

You know what? If your child *were* to work in a commercial without being paid, believe me, you would eventually resent it. So don't even think of doing it.

By the way, agents earn 10% commissions, managers earn 15%.

I've included an extensive list of the biggest and best personal managers and franchised agents in chapters 11 and 10.

I've also listed the branch offices of the major show business unions, to which you can write for a list of franchised agents in your area, in chapter 20.

If you do so, please enclose a legal-sized, self-addressed, stamped envelope. These organizations are nonprofit; this will make it easier (and less expensive) for them to give you all the information you need.

Casting Directors

Casting directors are hired by the producer of a play, film, commercial, or television show to recommend performers for specific roles. Sometimes casting directors will have one day to cast a project. Sometimes they'll have several weeks. However long they have, their search always begins in the same way—with head shots. (If a casting director is working on a commercial, they won't use head shots.)

The casting director calls several agents and tells each of them, "I'm working on a Levi's 501 Jeans commercial and I need children between the ages of fifteen to eighteen, all colors, all sizes, all shapes. My interviews will be tomorrow. Give me no more than three names, because I'm only going to be working on this project for a couple of hours tomorrow, and I only have time to see fifteen children."

That's when the agents call the managers and my part of the procedure begins. I've already explained how I get a commercial breakdown and what I do. Is there a difference between the way a commercial and a legit project is cast? Absolutely.

If it is a legit project, the casting director will send out a written breakdown of the entire project to every agent on both coasts. The agents will carefully read this to identify not just the physical characteristics of the role, but the "personality" requirements—a breakdown of a legit project goes into far more detail on each character, not just hair color, gender and age.

The casting director may well want pictures of potential players immediately. My office is about an hour from Manhattan, where all the agents I deal with on the East Coast are located. An agent may call me and say, "We're working on a feature film and I need dark-haired five-year-old boys; the character is a sensitive, withdrawn child," and go into whatever other details they have on the character. If I feel that I have one or two children who really fit that particular role, then I will messenger or fax the head shots to the agent.

So twenty-four hours later, the casting director is sitting there with all these head shots, and believe me, they must get hundreds. If the casting director picks up a picture and thinks, "Wow, this kid looks just like the character," he calls the agent and says, "You sent me a picture of Bobby Green. I would like to see this little boy in my office tomorrow. I think he looks exactly like the little boy in the script."

If Bobby Green is *your* little boy, the casting director will make sure that your child is given a script. You, your child and the manager will probably work on the script as quickly as possible, aiming to give your child a real command of the character.

The next day at the appointed time, your child goes into the casting director's office and performs the script, which, of course, he's memorized. If the casting director feels your child did an excellent job and really is exactly what they're looking for, he will be called back to read for the producer.

(We've also used this term throughout the book. What are the odds of getting a callback? If a casting director sees forty children for a particular role, she will probably narrow the choice down to ten. These ten children will come back and perform again, but on videotape. This videotape is then presented to the producer. After the producer looks at the tapes, he and the casting director together will attend a second callback. Three of the original 40 children will be at this second callback. It is after this session that the final decision is made.)

Casting directors are independent—they work at the whim of producers. So it is very much in the casting director's favor to find the perfect child for the role. If she does so, she will most likely be used again and again by that producer.

So the casting director will, in many instances, work with the three children still in the running. She will make sure that they dress according to the role, that they show up on time, that they understand the character. Maybe she will work on the script with them, perhaps to give them a different perspective than the one they have. It is her job to make sure that her producer *loves* the people she sends them.

That Stranger Could Be A Casting Director

Casting directors are always looking for talented children. They make sure that they attend as many productions as possible. I know casting directors in New York who go to a different show every evening. Some casting directors may make the rounds of the local high schools and see their productions. Many times a casting director will call me and say, "I recently attended a production at a local studio and came across a child that I feel you should contact. I feel this child is extremely talented. I spoke with the mother and told her the child needs representation. I gave her your card and she will be contacting you."

I get a lot of referrals from casting directors because they are not in a position to represent talent. Their job is to present talent to the producers. I always feel that it's a good idea to send your head shot out to a casting director. If she's working on a project, and she remembers that picture and pulls it out, believe me, she will contact you. (Independent casting directors on both coasts are listed in chapter 13. Major New York advertising agency casting directors are listed in chapter 12.)

I wrote this book to help you prepare your child for a career in show business. That career can only become a reality if you find the right person to guide you.

Remember, legitimate agents, managers, casting directors, and producers do not charge *any* up-front money. If they do, RUN, do not walk, out of their offices! And if anyone says to you, "Well, you have a very cute child, but I don't like these pictures you took. Go to my photographer," just tell them to forget it. They should be able to work with the pictures that you presented them. There are a lot of people out there who are looking to take advantage of parents. Nobody should make money unless your child works. It's that simple.

Equally important, remember that a personal manager or an agent cannot do your job as a parent, but *you* can't do the job of the professional, either. Both you and the manager are key to the success of your child. Only you know your child and how to motivate him; only the professional knows how to protect him and guide you through difficult decisions that will constantly pop up in the life of a successful child.

Whenever I interview a child for the first time and I feel that I would like to represent him, my first question to the parents is always, "Have you seen other legitimate managers or agents in the industry?" If the answer is no, I encourage them to do so—it's the only way an objective decision can be made as to whom will represent your child. As far as I'm concerned, having parents want me to represent their child at the same time that I also want to represent them gets our relationship off to an excellent start.

Is it really necessary for you to pay out those commissions to a manager? Couldn't you just do it all yourself and pocket them yourself? I wouldn't recommend it, and I'm not saying that because I am a manager. The reality is that you couldn't possibly begin to guess at the hundreds of things that come up, let alone how to handle them. Were you representing your own child, devastating results could happen.

Are you aware of the different laws governing children for each state? Would you know the difference between union and non-union regulations? Could you be certain that your child was getting paid exactly what he was entitled to? Would you know when additional compensation for particular situations was appropriate? Would you know what projects to turn down in order to make correct career moves? Can you tell if someone is taking advantage of your child, and not be fooled by sincerity?

If your child started working, would you know what conflicts each commercial held? For example, if your child were to do a Burger King commercial, she would not be allowed to do any other fast-food commercials. They would be considered conflicts. It's important to know this before you accept *any* commercial—you may actually turn one down to allow your child to land a bigger and better one in the same category!

As I said before, show business is a wonderful career for children—they could probably have college paid for with a few national commercials; they could even become major stars earning in the millions.

Do your part, and let the professional do theirs.

The bottom line is to TRUST and HAVE CONFIDENCE in the person who will be representing your child. Working together, each of you in your specific roles, guarantees success.

Everyone working together.

Chapter
8

Meeting And Greeting

So far, it's been real easy, right? You shot your child's head shots yourself. You weren't nervous, they came out great, and you're thrilled. You've had them reproduced. You finished his resume. Now you're sitting there with all these beautiful head shots and resumes and you're thinking, "Okay, I'm ready. Let's go, let's go."

Hauling The Mail Bags

You're ready to inundate the industry with your child's head shots. Be prepared to get responses, because you will. Be prepared to have your child asked to come in for interviews and to start taking your child out on auditions.

You've gotten together a list of the managers, agents and casting directors to whom you're going to mail out your head shots. Make sure that the resume is attached to each head shot neatly and that it doesn't hang over the edge. Put the picture into a large envelope, hand print your return address, and hand print the address that it's going to. Make sure you apply the correct amount of postage.

You may be sending pictures all over the country. How are you going to find out what all those pros think of your little darling? It's going to be very difficult (not to mention expensive) for you to call everybody. And, as we've discussed, most managers, let alone agents and casting directors, are far too busy and do not welcome calls from non-clients asking questions. I know I get calls all the time from parents asking me, "Did you receive my child's picture? What do you think? Do you want to see the child?" I receive more than a hundred pictures a week—it's virtually impossible to remember whom I've seen in person, let alone whom I've seen pictures of!

I've devised a simple method, using postcards, that will give you the answers you're seeking without spending a lot of money or time. (See the sample reproduced on page 101.) This postcard is addressed to yourself—the name and address of the agent, manager, or casting director to whom you've sent a head shot goes in the return address section. Print as many postcards as you have head shots and enclose one—*stamped* —with every head shot you send out. You can be sure, if all a manager has to do is check a box and stick the postcard in the mail, he probably will.

There are four boxes he or she can check:

- "We would like to set up an appointment to meet with your child. Please call our office." (You've left room for the manager to put his or her phone number. How fast can you get to the phone? They are interested!)
- "We are not interviewing for new clients at this time." (This could be the truth; it could also be a

general brush-off. If it's the truth, things change
—but you'll never know when they start interviewing again...unless you stay in touch.)
- "We do not represent performers in your child's
  age range. Please contact us when your child has
  reached the age of ____."
- "We are keeping your child's photo on file for
  future reference." (Maybe another brush-off, but
  who knows? Again, stay in touch.)

These four boxes cover every response an agent or a manager can have to a picture of your child. Don't think that if you
don't hear from somebody, they don't like your child. Chances
are they love your child, but they may not have an immediate
need for her or the time to devote to her. Or they may already
have someone working who is very similar to your child.

For example, my personal policy is that I only represent
one or two children in each age range—I will not cause any
competition within my own agency. I may receive a head shot
of a little five-year-old girl who is blue-eyed and blonde...and
looks exactly like the little girl I now represent. If I would
have contacted that child barring a conflict, I will *not* discard
that head shot. My own client may get ill or decide to stop
working. She may take a vacation or be working on a film that
ties her up for six months. If or when something like that
happens, I will set up an appointment to meet the new child.

Some people suggest you enclose a cover letter with each
head shot. When I get a picture with a cover letter, I look at
the picture first. If I like what I see, I turn it over to see the
child's vital statistics and the type of training and experience
the child has had. If I'm *still* interested in having the child
come in for an interview, I *may* read the cover letter.

In other words, I don't think a cover letter is important.
It's the head shot and resume that counts. But what *is* important, is that you enclose a self-addressed stamped envelope if

Sample Postcard

Front

```
                                              ┌──────┐
                                              │Affix │
                                              │Stamp │
                                              │Here  │
                                              └──────┘

John Doe, Casting Director
Big Talent, Inc.
666 Anywhere,
Anytown, CA 90000


              Your Name
              Your Street Address
              Your City, State, Zip
```

Back

- ❑ We would like to set up an appointment to meet with your child. Please call our office." (And, of course, you've left room for the manager to put his or her phone number.)
- ❑ We are not interviewing for new clients at this time."
- ❑ We do not represent performers in your child's age range. Please contact us when your child has reached the age of ____."
- ❑ We are keeping your child's photo on file for future reference."

you want your picture back (and, of course, the stamped post-card I've suggested if you want to know my response). Many times I receive color pictures and beautifully printed resumes that I'm sure the parents would like returned. Without a stamped envelope, it's extremely difficult (and expensive) for me to return pictures. I probably won't.

I get at least three to four phone calls every day from parents asking me what I thought of their pictures. Do I think their child had potential for show business? Sometimes I don't even get pictures of children, just letters from parents describing their children and asking me if I think they have potential. I have to be honest with you—there is absolutely nothing I can tell from a photograph except that I think the child is adorable. Do I have room in my agency for this child's age range? That's really what I base my criteria on.

I never single out a child because the child is not good looking. To some extent, I don't care what the child looks like—I need a child whom I feel is animated. That's what I'm looking for in a photograph. If he's got a nice natural smile on his face, that's all that counts. If I'm looking for that age range, I'd probably have the child come in to interview.

Follow Up, Follow Up, Follow Up

You've sent out your head shots. You've enclosed your postcards and your self-addressed stamped envelopes. Now you wait.

But don't wait too long. In this business, follow-up is very important. Keep sending pictures out. You have to be persistent and consistent. For diversity's sake, you may want to follow up with a picture postcard—postcard-size pictures with your child's picture and phone number on the front, perhaps with a little note on the back saying, "I recently sent you my child's head shot and resume. Would you be interested in seeing this child? He still does not have representation." (See chapter 6 for a discussion of pertinent prices for picture postcards.)

If your child has gotten any kind of a job, you can also use these picture postcards to invite the manager or agent to see your child in person: "I recently sent you a picture and resume of my child. She is currently working in a fashion show at Buy 'Em Up Mall. Do you have the time to come see her?"

Or, "My child is appearing in a local production of 'The King and I'. Could you attend an October 21 performance? Tickets are complimentary. Please call and we will have them at the door for you." (Don't forget, of course, to buy the tickets and leave them! And don't ever think of *not* paying for them yourself.)

What you're trying to do is get your child seen by as many people as possible. Please, don't automatically assume that the person you are mailing the pictures to is not interested in your child if you have not heard from him. As I said before, he may already represent someone who looks like your child. He may have too many children in your child's age range. He may not be interviewing any new children at this time. But when he decides that it's time to start interviewing new children again or when the clients he's had in your child's age range are no longer with him, your child's head shot or picture postcard may show up at just the right time.

More than once, for example, I've gotten a picture of a child, and for some reason, decided I wasn't interested. A few weeks later I got another picture. Four weeks later, a postcard. A few weeks later, another postcard.

When this happens, I invariably wind up admiring the parents' persistence. They have shown they're serious and dedicated to their child's potential career—an important factor—but they haven't been pests. They had the good sense, for example, not to call me, which can be very disruptive. After this kind of follow-up, I will inevitably have that child come in for an interview—and I know that my colleagues feel the same way.

So remember: Do not call. Do everything by mail. Make it as easy as possible for the agent or manager to respond to you. Enclose a self-addressed stamped envelope, a picture postcard, a regular postcard.

And don't give up. We all respect persistence if it's done the right way.

Time To Organize

It's very important to keep complete and careful records of whom you've sent head shots and when—you don't want to send them every week to the same people. That's too often. Agents and managers receive hundreds of pictures every week, and we might well be two or three weeks behind going through them. Be patient. I would follow up every six to eight weeks.

Keep records of the replies you receive.

Keep a record of the times and dates of interviews and auditions.

Keep track of the car fare to auditions and any other expenses involved in your child's career. When your child starts to earn money, you can start reimbursing yourself for your initial expenses—travel, pictures, resumes, lessons, postage, telephone calls, etc.

When The Phone Starts Ringing

Once you start getting responses to your child's head shots, and agents and managers start setting up appointments to meet your child, see as many people as you can. Selecting that one person who will be guiding your child's career requires a tremendous commitment on both your parts, a commitment that may last for years. Don't be unfair to yourself or your child—don't make such a commitment unless you are totally convinced that the person who will be representing your child is the person you want.

Don't be fooled by fast talkers or impressive client lists. If somebody tells you he represents this big star and that big star, don't let that fool you. These same people may have 400 people on their roster, but spend 90 percent of their time working for the star clients. What happens to the rest? Anyone representing large numbers of people couldn't possibly do a personalized job for your child.

You Only Get One Chance

An agent or manager may try to contact you by phone. Either make sure that you are always home and that your phone is never busy, purchase an answering machine, or hire an answering service. You *don't* want to miss a call. Very rarely will I call twice. It's very frustrating to have a certain amount of time to submit names or to get a certain number of children into an audition. If I've called and you're not there, I will go on to the next person. You have to be able to be accessible to the people who will be calling you.

If you purchase an answering machine, get one with a "remote" feature, which will allow you to pick up your messages while you're away from home. As I said before, expect collect calls. That's the business. (There are ways to keep your expenses down in this regard, since collect calls are very expensive. I call my clients who live out of town collect, they tell the operator they do not accept collect calls, and then they call me back.)

Before You Sign Away Your Life...

WHEN SOMEONE OFFERS YOU A CONTRACT, DO NOT SIGN IT BEFORE YOU READ IT. Make sure you completely understand all the terms. Consult an attorney. Don't let anyone pressure you into anything. Once you become a member of one of the unions, any contracts you are offered can be sent to the union and they will look them over for you and advise you whether they're good or not.

The working relationship between you and your child's manager has to be one that is very comfortable for all of you. Being a mother, for example, I understand that you have other obligations. I would never call one of my clients and say, "Take your child on this audition." I always present it in this manner, "There is an audition tomorrow at 4:00 p.m. for a Macy's catalog shoot. Can you take your child?" If you say no, fine. Probably the worst thing that could happen is that you will say "no" several times in a row. I'll just stop calling you, presuming that you just don't want to do this any longer.

And that's okay. This business isn't for everyone. And all of you need to keep your life and your children's lives in perspective.

Even if your child is successful, occasional time off may be called for. Children need time to play. Children need time for friends. I don't think that a child should do this work twenty-four hours a day. There is time for this business, and there is time to just be a kid. As a parent, you must choose the balance best for your child. Virtually all of the successful children I know in this business have very well-rounded lives, lives that are evenly balanced between play time, work time, school time, and family time.

It is totally up to you how much you involve your child in this business. You can have a successful child, whatever your decision.

Chapter
9

Where The Action Is

Opportunities On Both Coasts

Both New York and Los Angeles offer the most opportunities for children in this industry. Please don't let that discourage you if you do not live within a reasonable commuting distance.

(Later in this chapter, I will discuss how you can get your child started in this business without having to relocate to one of its two centers, no matter where you live.)

However, for those of you who do live within driving distance of New York or L.A., let me give you an idea of what you can expect.

The majority of commercials are shot in New York. And those that are not shot there usually are *created* there—by one of the many advertising agencies New York is known for.

New York is also known for it's theater. The Great White Way—Broadway—is the center of New York's theater world, though fewer than two dozen theaters actually make up "Broadway." But there are hundreds of off-Broadway and off-off Broadway theaters. (See chapter 14 for a complete listing.) And hundreds more cabaret clubs, nightclubs and showcases where aspiring singers, dancers and actors can show off their talents.

New York also produces the majority of the soap operas with which many of you are familiar.

Los Angeles is where the major television networks create the situation comedies ("sitcoms"), made-for-TV movies, and series that make up most of prime time. Though some may be shot in New York (and other cities), the casting is done in L. A.

Children have tremendous opportunities on both coasts, but the competition in these two power centers is equally tremendous.

The Coogan Law And Other Rules

Both coasts have different rules and regulations concerning child actors. Familiarizing yourself with these differences will help you decide whether or not relocating is a viable idea for you at the present time.

The "Coogan Law" was named after Jackie Coogan, a child star of the '20s and '30s who made lots of money as a well-known child actor (he was the Kid in the original "The Champ," with Wallace Beery) only to find out when he turned 21 that most of it had been spent by his parents.

The states that have a Coogan Law—and California is one—withhold a percentage of the money a child earns and keep it in trust until he or she reaches adulthood. Many of my clients now working in L.A. have as much as 30% taken out of their gross earnings. By the time taxes and commissions are extracted from what remains, sometimes there isn't a lot left over. This is a major consideration if you are thinking of moving to L.A. to begin a career. Frankly, despite the occasional difficulty it presents for some parents, I like the Coogan Law —it's forced savings for the child.

New York handles things differently. All monies the child earns are given to the parents.

Work permits are necessary on both coasts. In New York, a separate work permit is required for each particular job. In L.A., a general work permit—good for one year—is required. If the work permit expires and your child has booked a commercial, there is no way that the child can work in the state of California.

When children work in L.A., tutors are always on the sets. They not only teach the child, but are responsible for the health, safety and welfare of all children under the age of 16. A tutor can refuse to allow a child to work on a set or location which he or she feels jeopardizes the child's health, safety or morals.

New York's rules are quite different. Tutors are not always provided, nor are they required. It is the responsibility of the parent to make sure the child's school work is kept up.

Both coasts abide by the strict regulations set by the unions, which is another reason why professional representation is so important. Only a professional can insure you that your child will be working with the most legitimate producers in the industry, and that they will be treated appropriately.

Meanwhile, Away From The Coasts

You're sitting there and your saying to yourself, "Well, I live in a small town out in the middle of nowhere. I just called the National Conference of Personal Managers—there are no members in my area. I called SAG (Screen Actors Guild), AFTRA (American Federation of Television and Radio Artists) and AEA (Actors Equity Association) and there are no franchised agents in my area. What do I do now? Does that mean that I have absolutely no chance of getting my child into show business unless I move to a big city?"

No! You can get your child involved in show business no matter where you live, and I don't mean that you have to travel 300 miles every day to get your child to an audition. You're going to start off locally, where there is probably so much work to be done that you could be kept quite busy every day of the year if you chose.

You do not, I repeat, *not,* have to live in a big city to get your child work in this industry. There are plenty of opportunities, even in the smallest towns. All it takes is some creative research

Start off with the phone book. Look under "Advertising Agencies." Even in smaller towns, you'll find several ad agencies listed. Call them and ask to speak to their art director or whoever does the casting for the local television commercials or print advertisements. Local advertising agencies are always looking for children to do print advertisements, and many of them produce all the local radio and television commercials.

Now turn to the "Department Store" listings. Contact them, ask the store to connect you with their photography division (and make sure it's not the photography department that does portraits of children for family use). If the operator tells you that they don't have a photography department, ask for the name of the agency that does their store's advertisements. If they say they don't use an advertising agency, ask for the name of the freelance photographer who shoots the advertisements. One of these three will get you in touch with whomever actually "casts" the ads.

Ask to be put in touch with somebody who handles their special events. A lot of the major department stores in New York have a special events department that handles their fashion shows. This is an excellent way for children to get some experience. (Smaller stores may not have a department, but may still have someone coordinating shows. Find her.)

Contact some of the local malls—they also put on fashion shows. Any store in the shopping mall can direct you to the mall headquarters office. Find out who produces these fashion shows.

The producers of films being shot in your area may well be seeking extras, in which case they will usually print casting notices in the local newspapers. Extra work is an excellent opportunity for your child to earn some money while gaining firsthand experience on a movie set.

Every state now has a film board which encourages film companies to use their states for movie locations. To get in touch with the film board, call your local town hall. I'm sure they will be able to get you in touch with your state film board. Write a letter, asking which production companies will be shooting in your area in the future. They may also have a listing of the casting directors for these productions.

Check with local churches and synagogues—community theater groups usually use the facilities of these institutions to put on plays.

Get in touch with local colleges. Sometimes professional touring companies use the facilities of local colleges for their productions and use local talent in small roles.

A touring company is a group of actors that go from one town or city to another presenting plays—while they keep the major roles for themselves, the small roles are generally filled by people in each town they visit.

Are there any major corporations in your area? Many such companies produce industrial films and sometimes cast the entire production using local actors. (I've listed the major industrial production companies in chapter 18.)

In the summertime, amusement parks do their own casting for the small reviews that they present. Remember the little groups singing, or dancing, or putting on skits at last summer's carnival? Where are those singers, dancers and actors coming from?

Get in touch with the parks before the season opens—if they are looking for performers, they'll let you know. (I've listed the big theme parks across the country—and those individuals responsible for casting their shows—in chapter 19.)

Get in touch with the drama departments at local high schools. Drama teachers are often involved in community theater. Ask them where you can find casting information for local theater groups.

(I've also listed the resident theaters, equity and non-equity theaters throughout the country in chapters 15, 16 & 17, respectively.)

Several years ago, *Sixteen* magazine did an article on my agency. Because it's an international publication, I received letters from teenagers all over the world asking me how they could get into show business.

I remember one particular letter that I received from a little girl in Brazil. She lived in a very small town, was thirteen years old, and wanted to get into show business. Could I give her any advice?

I wrote to her and gave her all the information that I just gave you. Unfortunately, she lived in such a small, poor town that none of my advice was pertinent—there were no local productions, no malls, no ad agencies, no advertising! And both her parents were totally unavailable to take her to the larger town twenty miles away where she may have done some print ads for a local store.

I suggested that she approach her local church about putting on a talent show with some of her friends. I suggested she tell the pastor that if he would let them put on a show, any money they raised would be donated to the church.

She wrote back to tell me that about 200 people showed up at the church, the church collected a very nice sum of money, and they were thrilled. The show was a success. It gave her a chance to be a part of show business, even though it was on a small scale.

There's always something you can do. So do some creative thinking!

If you want your child in show business, this book and your persistence will help you reach your goal.

Section Three

Action!

The Contacts You Need To Succeed

Chapter 10

Children's Agents - My Choice

East Coast Agents

Abrams Artists & Associates, Inc.
420 Madison Avenue—Suite 1400
New York, NY 10017
212/935-8980

Agents: Robert McCarthy,
Deborah Levy

Agents for the Arts, Inc.
1650 Broadway—Suite 306
New York, NY 10019
212/247-3220

Agent: Scott McNulty

Andreadis Talent
119 West 57th Street—Suite 813
New York, NY 10019
212/315-0303

Agent: Barbara Andreadis

J. Michael Bloom
233 Park Avenue South
New York, NY 10003
212/529-5800 or 529-6500

Agent: Barbara Coleman-
DiMarco

Don Buchwald & Assoc.,Inc.
10 East 44th Street
New York, NY 10017
212/867-1200

Carson Adler Agency
250 West 57th Street
New York, NY 10107
212/307-1882

Marje Fields
165 West 46th Street
New York, NY 10036
212/764-5740
Agent: Lee Buckler

Ford Children's Division
344 East 59th Street
New York, NY 10022
212/688-8628
Agents: Barbara Laga, Lois Williams

Frontier Booking Int'l.
1776 Broadway
New York, NY 10019
212/265-0822
Agent: Lisa Weinberg

Gilchrist Talent Group, Inc.
310 Madison Avenue—Suite 1003
New York, NY 10017
212/692-9166

Michael Hartig Agency, Ltd.
114 East 28th Street
New York, NY 10016
212/684-0010

Henderson/Hogan Agency, Inc.
405 West 44th Street
New York, NY 10036
212/765-5190
Agent: Jean Walton

Jan J. Agency, Inc.
328 East 61st Street
New York, NY 10021
212/759-9775
Agents: Jan Jarrett, David Eisenberg

Joe Jordan Talent Agency, Inc.
156 Fifth Avenue—Suite 711
New York, NY 10010
212/463-8455
Agents: Robin Dornbaum, Jeffrey J. Gill

The Sanders Agency, Ltd.
1204 Broadway
New York, NY 10001
212/779-3737

Schiffman, Ekman, Morrison & Marx, Inc.
156 Fifth Avenue—Suite 523
New York, NY 10010
212/627-5500
Agents: Elana Barry, John Shea

West Coast Agents

Bloom & Associates
9200 Sunset Blvd., #710
Los Angeles, CA 90069
213/275-8800
Agents: J. Michael Bloom, Robert Risher, Joel Millner, Ric Beddingfield, Marilyn Szatmary, Nancy Jones

Booh Schut Agency
11350 Ventura Blvd., Suite 206
Studio City, CA 91604
818/760-6680

Iris Burton Agency
1450 Belfast Drive
Los Angeles, CA 90069
213/652-0964

Harry Gold and Associates
12725 Ventura Blvd., #E
Studio City, CA 91604
818/789-5003

Agents: Harry Gold, Joy Stevenson, Ben Frieberger, Ruth Hansen, Francine Gersh

Kelman/Arletta & Assoc.
7813 Sunset Blvd.
Los Angeles, CA 90046
213/851-8822

Agents: Arletta Proch, Susie Mains

Tyler Kjar Agency
8961 Sunset Blvd., #B
Los Angeles, CA 90069
213/278-0912

Agents: Tyler Kjar, Brandon Kjar, Candy Rouse, Pam Kelley

Natalie Rosson Agency
11712 Moorpark Street, #205B
Studio City, CA 91604
818/508-1445

Agent: Natalie Rosson

Twentieth Century Artists
3800 Barham Blvd., #303
Los Angeles, CA 90068
213/850-5516

Agents: Diane Davis, Vivian Hollander, Jerry Davidson Steven R. Stevens, Estelle Hertzberg, Cindi Davis, Stevie Nelson

Chapter 11

Personal Managers

These managers all belong to the highly regarded National Conference of Personal Managers, whose ethical standards assure you of their competence.

East Coast Chapter

1650 Broadway—Suite 705
New York, NY 10019
212/265-3366
Joseph Rapp

East Coast Members

Connections
45 Lawson Drive
Madison, CT 06443
203/245-4448
Peggy Adler Robohm

Cuzzins Management
250 West 57th Street—Suite 1632
New York, NY 10019
212/586-1573
Helene Sokol

Discovery Talent Mgnt., Ltd.
72 Moriches Road
Lake Grove, NY 11755
212/308-0930
Estelle Fusco

Michele Donay Talent Mgnt.
236 East 74th Street
New York, NY 10021
212/744-9406
Michele Donay

Scott Eden Creative Management
4 Vails Lane
Millwood, NY 10546
914/941-8684 or 212/953-1379
Martin Siegel

Fox-Albert Management Ent., Inc.
1697 Broadway—Suite 1210
New York, NY 10019
212/581-1011
Jean T. Fox, Adrienne Albert

Victoria Frankmano
84-01 53rd Avenue
Elmhurst, NY 11373
212/593-4764 or 718/478-2801

Fresh Faces Management, Inc.
2911 Carnation Avenue
Baldwin, NY 11510
516/223-0034
Aggie Gold

Gekis Management
240 West 44th Street—Suite 8
New York, NY 10036
212/302-2556
Theodors Gekis

Goldstar Talent Management
246 Fifth Avenue—Suite 202
New York, NY 10001
212/213-1707
Sid Gold

John N. Jennings
881 10th Avenue—Suite 1A
New York, NY 10019
212/581-0377 or 201/224-5974

Jennifer Lambert
1600 Broadway—Suite 1001
New York, NY 10019
212/315-0665 or 315-0754

McGovern/Goodwin Theatrical
Management
Nine Layton Avenue
Hicksville, NY 11801
212/860-7400 or 516/681-2723
Arline McGovern, Lois Goodwin

J. Mitchell Management
88 Bleeker Street, Ste. 2H, #29
New York, NY 10012
212/777-6686
Jeff Mitchell

Donna Mollo
1143 West Broadway
Hewlett, NY 11557
516/569-3253

Moore Entertainment Group
11 Possum Trail
Upper Saddle River, NJ 07458
201/327-3698
Barbara Moore

New Personalities, Inc.
272-60 Grand Central Parkway
Floral Park, NY 11005
718/631-3636
Mark Belsky

Cathy Parker Management, Inc.
P.O. Box 716
Voorhees TWP, NJ 08043
609/354-2020 or 800/872-5252
Cathy Parker

Podesoir International Mngt.
401 Schenectady Ave.—Suite 7E
Brooklyn, NY 11213
718/756-4016
K. Charisse Dicks

Edie Robb Talent Works, Inc.
301 West 53rd Street—Suite 4K
New York, NY 10019
212/245-3250 or 215/947-5361
Charles Worthington, Edie Robb

Sea-Management
51 East 42nd Street
New York, NY 10017
212/697-9840 or 914/763-8014

Suzelle Enterprises
182-06 Midland Parkway
Jamaica Estates, NY 11432
718/380-0585
Suzanne Schachter

Talent & Comedy Management
3 Adam Street
Floral Park, NY 11001
718/343-9530
Joan M. Rosenberg

World of Culture, Ltd.
463 West Street—Suite 509
New York, NY 10014
212/243-0292
Mark Hall Amitin

Page Management
5315 Oakdale Avenue
Woodland Hills, CA 91364
818/703-7328
Jean Page

West Coast Chapter

4527 Park Allegra
Calabasa Park, CA 91302
818/888-8264
Tami Lynn, Executive Director

West Coast Members

Creative Mgnt. Network, Inc.
P.O. Box 3225
Hollywood, CA 90078
213/931-8353
Sandra Lord

Howard Hinderstein Production
6430 Sunset Blvd., #1018
Hollywood, CA 90028
213/262-7140 or 213/464-4300
Howard Hinderstein

Chapter 12

New York Ad Agency Casting Directors

Ally & Gargano, Inc.
805 Third Avenue
New York, NY 10022
212/688-5300

Casting directors: Rhoda Karp, Renee Howley, Maureen Chilton; assistant casting directors: Joe Ann Brennan, Janet Eisenberg, Marilyn Zitner; casting coordinator: Emily Norton.

Comments: Send pictures and resumes.

Batten, Barton, Durstine & Osborn, Inc.
1285 Avenue of the Americas
New York, NY 10019
212/459-6705

Heads of casting: Terry Berland, Cabrina Carnevale; assistant: Eileen A. Powers.

Comments: Pictures & resumes accepted; do not phone.

Leo Burnett Co. Inc.
950 Third Avenue
New York, NY 10022
212/759-5959

Comments: Casting through Leo Burnett USA, Prudential Plaza, Chicago, IL 60601

Campbell-Mithun-Esty
100 East 42nd Street
New York, NY 10017
212/692-6200

Casting director: Mary Tibaldi; associate casting director: Janine Minunno.

Comments: Pictures & resumes accepted; do not phone or visit.

D'Arcy Masius Benton & Bowles
909 Third Avenue
New York, NY 10022
212/758-6200

Casting director: Linda Ferrara; casting assistant: Susan Bastian.

Comments: Casts through files and agents; do not phone.

Grey Advertising, Inc.
777 Third Avenue
New York, NY 10017
212/546-2000

Vice president: Jerry Saviola; associate: Barbara Bennett, casting directors: Claudia Walden, Madeline Molnar, Michael O'Gara, Arista Baltronis, Dolores Fisher; casting assistants: Ted Sluberski, Lisa Weinberg.

Comments: Send pictures & resumes; no calls accepted.

Holland & Callaway
767 Third Avenue
New York, NY 10017
212/308-2750

Broadcast manager/casting: Carol Parrino, producers/casting: Arthur Wright, Russ Keiser.

Comments: Pictures & resumes accepted.

Jordan, McGrath, Case & Taylor
445 Park Avenue
New York, NY 10022
212/326-9100

Casting director: Vicki Goggin; assistant: Karen Apicella.

Comments: Accepts pictures & resumes.

Kornhauser & Calene, Inc.
228 East 45 Street
New York, NY 10017
212/490-1313

Head of production: Pamela Mayheny; assistants: Tracy Dennis, Janice Entwistel.

Comments: Casts through agents only; accepts pictures & resumes by mail; no phone calls.

Laurence, Charles, Free & Lawson, Inc.
260 Madison Avenue—4th Floor
New York, NY 10016
212/213-4646

Executive producer: Ellen Goldschmidt; casting director: Matthew Messinger.

Comments: Casts through agents only as required per commercial; accepts pictures & resumes from SAG extras only; no phone calls.

Lintas/NY
1 Dag Hammarskjold Plaza
New York, NY 10017
212/605-8290

VP: Steve Schaefer; casting supervisor: Barbara Blomberg, casting assistant: Susan Mattheiss.

Comments: Will call if needed; do not phone.

Lowe Marchalk Co., Inc.
1345 Avenue of the Americas
New York, NY 10105
212/708-8800

Casting director: Sharry Sabin.

Comments: Casts through agents only; no pictures or resumes accepted; no extras; do not phone.

McCann-Erickson USA
485 Lexington Avenue
New York, NY 10117
212/697-6000

Casting directors: John Cavoto, Jeannie Savino.
Comments: Send picture postcards only (no resumes or pictures); do not phone.

N.W. Ayer
Worldwide Plaza
825 Eighth Avenue
New York, NY 10019-7498

Senior VP/director of casting: Sally Howes Kandle.

Ogilvy & Mather
2 East 48 Street
New York, NY 10017
212/907-3400

Casting manager & VP: Daisy Sinclair; casting director; Barbara Herzog; print casting director: J.B. Sutherland; assistant: Kelly Barlow.
Comments: Casting and interviews done through agents and files only; accepts pictures & resumes for extras; do not phone.

Rosenfeld, Sirowitz, Humphrey & Strauss, Inc.
111 Fifth Avenue
New York, NY 10003
212/505-0200

Casting director: Judy Keller; producers: James Sircus, Ross Kronman.
Comments: Casts through agents and files; send pictures & resumes; do not phone.

Saatchi & Saatchi Advertising
375 Hudson Street
New York, NY 10014
212/463-2000

Casting directors: Leslee Feldman, Tina Sperber; assistants: Kirsten Walther, Debi Gochman.
Comments: Send resumes & pictures for extra work.

J. Walter Thompson Co.
466 Lexington Avenue
New York, NY 10017
212/210-7000

Casting director: Evangeline Hayes; second assistant casting director: Heather Aust.
Comments: Scale casting done by production firms and independent casting directors. Principal, overscale and voice-over casting done by the agency. Voice-over tapes accepted.

Young & Rubicam, Inc.
285 Madison Avenue
New York, NY 10017
212/210-3000

Senior VP/director of casting: Barbara Badyna; casting directors: Ann Batchelder, Sybil Trent, Cindy Bielak, Janet Shahbenderian; talent negotiator: Brenda Bareika; assistants: Sue Barnes, Thomas Winslow.
Comments: Send resumes & pictures for extra work; do not phone.

Chapter 13

Independent Casting Directors

There are no phone numbers included in this listing since most offices request that initial contact be made only by mail. Send pictures and/or resumes.

New York City

Joseph Abaldo Casting
450 West 42nd Street
New York, NY 10036

Deborah Aquila Casting
1633 Broadway—Suite1801
New York, NY 10019

Jay Binder Casting
513 West 54th Street
New York, NY 10019

Jane Brinker
513 West 54th Street
New York, NY 10019

Deborah Brown Casting
250 West 57th Street
New York, NY 10107

Madelyn J. Burns Casting
121 West 27th Street—Suite 503
New York, NY 10001

Kate Burton
39 West 19th Street
New York, NY 10011

Don Case Casting
8 East 12th St.
New York, NY 10010

Cast-Away! Casting Service
14 Sutton Place South
New York, NY 10022

Claire/Casting
333 Park Avenue South
New York, NY 10010

Complete Casting
240 West 44th Street
New York, NY 10036
(mailing address only)

Contemporary Casting, Ltd.
41 East 57th Street—Suite 901
New York, NY 10022

Creative Casting
1375 Broadway
New York, NY 10018

CTP Casting
22 West 27th Street
New York, NY 10001

Merry L. Delmonte Casting
& Production Co.
460 West 42nd Street
New York, NY 10036

Donna De Seta Casting
424 West 33rd Street
New York, NY 10001

Lou Digiaimo Assoc., Ltd.
P.O. Box 4296, FDR Station
New York, NY 10150

Sylvia Fay
71 Park Avenue
New York, NY 10016

Leonard Finger
1501 Broadway—Room 1511
New York, NY 10036

Maureen Fremont Casting
641 West 59th Street—Room 21
New York, NY 10019

Godlove, Serow, Sindlinger Casting
151 West 25th Street
New York, NY 10001

Golden Casting
133 West 72nd Street—Room 601
New York, NY 10023

Maria Greco Associates
1261 Broadway—Suite 308
New York, NY 10001

Judy Henderson & Assoc. Casting
330 West 89th Street
New York, NY 10024

Herman & Lipson Casting
24 West 25th Street
New York, NY 10010

Stuart Howard Assoc., Ltd.
22 West 27th St.
New York, NY 10010

Hughes Moss Casting
165 West 46th Street—Suite 700
New York, NY 10036

Hyde-Hamlet Casting
165 West 46th Street—Room 1115
New York, NY 10036

Kasha/Liebhart
275 Central Park West—Suite 2C
New York, NY 10024

Jack Kelly Casting
155 West 13th Street
New York, NY 10010

Jodi Kipperman Casts
211 Thompson Street—Suite 1C
New York, NY 10012

Lynn Kressel Casting
445 Park Avenue
New York, NY 10022

Lehner Stephens Casting
39 West 19th Street
New York, NY 10011

Joan Lynn Casting
39 West 19th Street
New York, NY 10011

McCorkle Casting Ltd.
264 West 40th Street—9th Floor
New York, NY 10018

Abigail McGrath, Inc.
1501 Broadway—Suite 1310
New York, NY 10036

MCL Casting, Ltd.
165 West 46th Street
New York, NY 10036

Elissa Myers
333 West 52nd Street
New York, NY 10019

Navarro/Bertoni Casting Co., Ltd.
101 West 31st Street—Room 2112
New York, NY 10001

Joanne Pasciuto, Inc.
1457 Broadway—Suite 308
New York, NY 10036

Jeff Passero
47 Perry Street—Suite 10
New York, NY 10014

Irma Puckett Casting
39 West 19th Street—12th Floor
New York, NY 10011

Reed & Melsky Casting
928 Broadway—Suite 300
New York, NY 10010

Reed/Sweeney/Reed Inc.
1780 Broadway
New York, NY 10019

Richmond Mussenden, Inc.
141 Fifth Avenue—Suite 5S
New York, NY 10019

Tony Roberts Casting Ltd.
150 Fifth Avenue
New York, NY 10011

Roelfs & Carroll Casting
(I.C.D.A.)
379 West Broadway—4th Floor
New York, NY 10012

Mike Roscoe Casting, Ltd.
153 East 37th Street—Suite 1B
New York, NY 10016

Sherie L. Seff Casting
400 West 43rd Street
New York, NY 10036

Barbara Shapiro
111 West 57th Street—Suite 1420
New York, NY 10019

Marcia Shulman
270 Lafayette Street
New York, NY 10012

Simon & Kumin Casting
1600 Broadway—Suite 609
New York, NY 10019

David Tochterman Casting
311 West 43rd Street—Suite 604
New York, NY 10036

Joy Todd, Inc.
Two West 32nd Street
New York, NY 10001

Joy Weber Casting
250 West 57th Street
New York, NY 10019

Susan Willett Casting
1170 Broadway—Suite 1008
New York, NY 10001

Bill Williams Casting
119 West 25th Street, PH
New York, NY 10001

Marji Camner Wollin & Assoc.
233 East 69th Street
New York, NY 10021

Ronnie Yeskel Casting
268 West 84th Street
New York, NY 10024

Jeffrey Zeiner
451 West 43rd Street
New York, NY 10036

Los Angeles

BCI (Barbara Claman)
6565 Sunset Blvd., #412
Los Angeles, CA 90028

Bengston/Cohn
11365 Ventura Blvd., #119
Studio City, CA 91604

Brown/West
7319 Beverly Blvd., #10
Los Angeles, CA 90036

Reuben Cannon & Assoc.
Paramount Studios
Gloria Swanson Bldg., #306
5555 Melrose Avenue
Los Angeles, CA 90038

The Casting Company
7319 Beverly Blvd., #One
Los Angeles, CA 90036

Champion/Basker Casting
7060 Hollywood Blvd., #808
Los Angeles, CA 90028

Rachelle Farberman
Kushner/Locke
10850 Wilshire Blvd.
Los Angeles, CA 90024

Fenton/Feinberg/Taylor Casting
Universal Studios
100 Universal City Plaza
Bungalow 477
Universal City, CA 91608

Henderson/Hanley Casting
8125 Lankershim Blvd.
North Hollywood, CA 91605

Judith Holstra Casting
3518 Cahuenga Blvd. West
Los Angeles, CA 90068

Caro Jones
5858 Hollywood Blvd.—Suite 220
Los Angeles, CA 90028

Liberman/Hirschfeld Casting
Sunset/Gower Studios
1438 North Gower Ave.—Ste. 1410
Los Angeles, CA 90028

McLean/Dimeo & Associates
12725 Ventura Blvd.—Suite H
Studio City, CA 91604

Bob Morones
733 North Seward Street
Los Angeles, CA 90038

Wallis Nicita & Assoc.
Paramount
5555 Melrose Avenue
Dressing Room Bldg., #200
Los Angeles, CA 90038

Onorato/Franks Casting
1717 N. Highland Avenue, #904
Los Angeles, CA 90028

Pagano/Bialy
1680 North Vine Street, #904
Los Angeles, CA 90028

The Part Company
7080 Hollywood Blvd., #606
Los Angeles, CA 90028

Penny Perry Casting
11350 Ventura Blvd., #210
Studio City, CA 91604

Barbara Remsen Casting
Raleigh Studios
650 North Bronson Avenue
Los Angeles, CA 90004

Lynn Stalmaster & Assoc.
9911 West Pico Blvd., #1580
Los Angeles, CA 90035

Chapter 14

Off- And Off-Off-Broadway Theater Companies

The About Face Company
442 West 42nd Street
New York, NY 10036
212/866-6737

Sean Burke, Richard Corley, Artistic Directors; Susan Geer, Production Director; Allison Jones, Managing Director

The Acting Company
P.O. Box 898
Times Square Station
New York, NY 10108
212/564-3510

Gerald Gutierrez, Artistic Director

The Acting Group
Box 1252—Old Chelsea Station
New York, NY 10011
212/645-1459

Celia Barrett, Prod. Artistic Dir

Actors' Alliance Inc.
J.A.F./P.O. Box 7370
New York, NY 10116
718/768-6110 or 805-0099

Melanie Sutherland, Juanita Walsh: Artistic Directors

Actors Outlet Theatre
120 West 28th Street
New York, NY 10001
212/645-0783 or 807-1590

Eleanor Segan, Executive Director; Ken Lowstetter, Artistic Director

Actors Repertory Theatre
303 East 44th Street
New York, NY 10017
212/687-6403

Warren Robertson, Artistic Director

The Actors' Space
250 West 54th Street—10th Fl.
New York, NY 10019
212/757-5900
Alan Langdon, Artistic Director

Alchemy Theater Company
515 East 85th Street
New York, NY 10028
212/744-4275
Gita Donovan, Artistic Director;
Geoffrey H. Dawe, Mnging Dir.

Amas Repertory Theatre
1 East 104th Street—3rd Floor
New York, NY 10029
212/369-8000
Rosetta LeNoire, Artistic Director

American Ensemble Company
P.O. Box 972—Peck Slip Station
New York, NY 10272
212/571-7594
Theatre address: 339 East 28th
Street, New York, NY 10016
Robert Petito, Artistic Director

American Folk Theatre
230 West 41st Street—Suite 1807
New York, NY 10036
212/391-2330; 757-0608 (box off.)
Dick Gaffield, Artistic Director

American Indian Community
Theatre Space
842 Broadway—8th Fl.
Theater Department
New York, NY 10003
212/598-0100
Gloria Miguel, Artistic Director

American Jewish Theatre
307 West 26th Street
New York, NY 10001
212/633-1588; 633-9797 (box off.)
Stanley Brechner, Artistic Director

The American Line
810 West 183rd Street, #5C
New York, NY 10033
212/740-9277
Richard Hoehler, Artistic Director;
Shakirah Wadud, Managing
Director

American Place Theatre, Inc.
111 West 46th Street
New York, NY 10036
212/840-2960
Wynn Handman, Artistic Director;
Mickey Rolfe, General Manager

American Playwrights Repertory
276 Fifth Avenue—Suite 505
New York, NY 10001
212/362-3964
Sarah Emory, Artistic Director

The American Renaissance
Theatre
112 Charlton Street
New York, NY 10014
212/929-4718
Susan Egert, Artistic Director

The American Stanislavski
Theatre
485 Park Avenue, #6A
New York, NY 10022
212/755-5120
Sonia Moore, Artistic Director

American Theatre of Actors
314 West 54th Street
New York, NY 10019
212/581-3044
James Jennings, Artistic Director

Any Place Theatre
P.O. Box 2467
New York, NY 10185
212/956-2384
Lynn Middleton, Artistic Director

Apple Corps Theatre
336 West 20th Street
New York, NY 1011
212/929-2955
John Raymond, Artistic Director

Art & Work Ensemble
870 6th Avenue
New York, NY 10001
212/213-0231
Anthony DiPietro, Artistic Director

Arts Club Theatre
8 East 3rd Street, #10
New York, NY 10003
212/673-5636
Linda Pakri, Artistic Director

Bare Stages
P.O. Box 6233
FDR Station
New York, NY 10150-1901
212/627-8495

Barrow Group
P.O. Box 2236
New York, NY 10108
212/512-1707
Seth Barrish, Artistic Director;
David Diamond, General Manager

Billie Holiday Theatre
1368 Fulton Street
Brooklyn, NY 11216
718/857-6363
Marjorie Moon, Producer

Black Spectrum Theatre Co.
119th Ave. & Merrick Blvd.
Jamaica, NY 11434
718/723-1800
Carl Clay, Artistic Director

Susan Bloch Theatre
307 West 26th Street
c/o Roundabout
100 East 17th Street
212/420-1360
Ellen Richard, General Manager

Blue Heron Theatre
645 West End Avenue
New York, NY 10025
212/787-0422
Ardelle Striker, Artistic Director

Bond Street Theatre Coalition
2 Bond Street
New York, NY 10012
212/254-4614
Joanna Sherman, Artistic Director

Bonk
P.O. Box 1776
Peter Stuyvesant Station
New York, NY 10009
Lisa Napoli, Artistic Director

Bread and Puppet Theater
c/o George Ashley
310 Greenwich Street, #31-A
New York, NY 10013
212/964-0263
George Ashley, Publicity

The Cab Theatre Co.
1729-31 1st Avenue, #5C
New York, NY 10128
212/996-1959
Joann Carollo, Managing Director

Cactus Theatre
91 Charles Street
New York, NY 10014
212/242-0709
Bo Brinkman, Artistic Director

Chicago City Limits
351 East 74th Street
New York, NY 10021
212/772-8707
Paul Zuckerman, Producer

Circle Repertory Company
161 Avenue of the Americas
New York, NY 10013
212/691-3210; 924-7100 (box off.)
Theater Address: 99 Seventh
Avenue S., New York, NY 10014
Tanya Berezin, Artistic Director

Circus Theatricals
711 West 171st Street, #67
New York, NY 10032
212/529-7794

Classic Theatre
200 Park Avenue
New York, NY 10166
212/636-4120
Maurice Edwards, Artistic
Director; Nicholas John Stathis,
Executive Director

Jean Cocteau Repertory
330 Bowery
New York, NY 10012
212/677-0060
Eve Adamson, Artistic Director

Common Ground
210 Forsyth Street
New York, NY 10002
212/505-6047
Norman Taffel, Artistic Director

Coney Island, USA
Boardwalk & W. 12th Street
Coney Island, NY 11224
718/372-5159
Dick Zigun, Artistic Director

Courtyard Players
P.O. Box 30952
Port Authority Sta.
New York, NY 10011
212/496-4288
Theater Address: 39 Grove Street,
New York, NY 10014
Bob Stark, Artistic Director

CSC Repertory, Ltd.
The Classic Stage Co.
136 East 13th Street
New York, NY 10003
212/677-4210
Carey Perloff, Artistic Director;
Ellen Novack, Managing Director

Dear Knows
263A West 19th Street—Suite 149
New York, NY 10011
212/691-9622
Paul Walker, Christopher Markle:
Artistic Directors

Double Image Theatre
444 West 56th Street—Room 1110
New York, NY 10019
212/245-2489
Helen Warren Mayer, Artistic Dir.

Drama Committee Rep. Theatre
118 West 79th Street
New York, NY 10024
212/595-1733

Dramatic Risks
60 East 4th Street, #19
New York, NY 10003

Eccentric Circles Theatre
c/o Hopkins
400 West 43rd Street, #4N
New York, NY 10036
Rosemary Hopkins, Paula Kay
Pierce, Janet Bruders, Barbara
Bunch: Artistic Directors

Economy Tires Theatre
DTW's Bessie Schonberg Theater
219 West 19th Street
New York, NY 10011
212/924-0077
David White, Executive Director

Elysium Theatre Company
P.O. Box 20521
Tompkins Square
New York, NY 10009
212/260-6114
Gregori Von Leitis, Artistic
Director

En Garde Arts
225 Rector Place—Suite 3A
New York, NY 10280
212/945-0336
Anne Hamburger, Producer

Ensemble Studio Theatre
549 West 52nd Street
New York, NY 10019
212/247-4982
Curt Dempster, Artistic Director

Equity Library Theatre
165 West 46th Street
New York, NY 10036
212/869-9266
Theater address: 310 Riverside Dr.
New York, NY 10025
212/663-2880
George Wojtasik, Producing
Director

The Family
9 Second Avenue—4th Fl.
New York, NY 10003
212/477-2522
J.J. Johnson, Artistic Director

The Firedrake Company
P.O. Box 400
Richmond Hill, NY 11418
718/849-4864
Joanna Andretta, David Gearino:
Co-Artistic Directors

Firing Squad/Comedy Rep Ensble
121 East 12th Street—Suite 7F
New York, NY 10003
212/473-0413
David Stamford, Producing Dir.;
Jackson Heath, Artistic Director

First Amendment Comedy Theatre
2 Bond Street
New York, NY 10012
212/473-1472
Barbara Contardi, Artistic Director

Folksbiene Theatre
123 East 55th Street
New York, NY 10022
212/888-0410
Ben Schechter, Artistic Director;
Morris Adler, Chairman

Fourth Wall Rep. Co.
79 East 4th Street
New York, NY 10003
212/254-5060
John Harvey, Artistic Director

Golden Fleece, Ltd.
204 West 20th Street
New York, NY 10011
212/691-6105
Lu Rodgers, Artistic Director

Hispanic Organization of Latin
Actors (HOLA)
250 West 65th Street
New York, NY 10023
212/595-8286
Francisco Rivela, Executive
Committee; Carlos Carrasco,
Artistic Director

Nat Horne Musical Theatre
440 West 42nd Street
New York, NY 10036
212/736-7128
Nat Horne, Chairman
(A membership organization. See
the About Face Co., Manhattan
Class Co., and Peter Samelson
Illusions.)

Hudson Guild Theatre
441 West 26th Street
New York, NY 10001
212/760-9810
Geoffrey Sherman, Artistic Director

Intar Hispanic American Theatre
P.O. Box 788
Times Square Station
New York, NY 10108
212/695-6134
Max Ferra, Artistic Director;
James Diapola, Managing
Director

Interart Theatre
549 West 52nd Street
New York, NY 10019
212/246-1050
Margot Lewitin, Artistic Director

Irish Arts Center
553 West 51st Street
New York, NY 10019
212/757-3319
Nye Heron, Producing Director;
Kurt Wagemann, General
Manager

Irondale Ensemble Project
782 West End Avenue
New York, NY 10025
212/666-7856; 633-1292
James Niesen, Artistic Director

Italian-American Rep. Theatre
496A Hudson Street—Suite E-25
New York, NY 10014
201/836-0907
Gene Ruffini, Artistic Director

Jewish Repertory Theatre
344 East 14th Street
New York, NY 10003
212/674-7200
Ran Avni, Artistic Director

La Mama Etc.
74-A East 4th Street
New York, NY 10009
212/475-7710
Wesley Jensby, Artistic Director;
Ellen Stewart, Founder

Lamb's Theatre Company
130 West 44th Street
New York, NY 10036
212/575-0300
Carolyn Rossi Copeland, Producing
Director

Latin American Theatre Ensemble
P.O. Box 1259, Radio City Station
New York, NY 10101
212.246-7478 or 410-4582
Theatre address: 172 East 104th St.
New York, NY 10029
Margarita Toirac, Executive
Director; Mario Pena, Margarita
Toirac, Founders

Lion Theatre Company
422 West 42nd Street
New York, NY 10036
212/736-7930

The Living Theatre
800 West End Avenue
New York, NY 10025
212/864-0516
Judith Malina, Hanon Reznikov:
Artistic Directors

Mabou Mines
150 First Avenue
New York, NY 10009
212/473-0559

Manhattan Arts Theatre, Film
& Video
145 West 46th St.—3rd Floor
New York, NY 10036
212/678-7550
Robert Mooney, Artistic Director

Manhattan Class Company
P.O. Box 279
Times Square Station
New York, NY 10108
212/239-9033
Theater Address: 442 West 42nd
Street, New York, NY 10036
Bob LuPone, Bernard Telsey:
Executive Directors

Manhattan Ensemble, Inc.
100 West 86th Street
New York, NY 10024
212/769-9240
Raymond Marciniak, Artistic
Director

Manhattan Punch Line
410 West 42nd Street—3rd Fl.
New York, NY 10036
212/239-0827
Steve Kaplan, Artistic Director

Manhattan Repertory Company
648 Broadway—Suite 700-B
New York, NY 10012
212/995-5582
Tom Chiodo, Peter DiPietro:
Artistic Directors
(Also owns Murder A LaCarte)

Manhattan Theater Club
453 West 16th Street
New York, NY 1011
212/645-5590
Lynne Meadow, Artistic Director

Mass Transit Street Theatre
c/o Robin Beall
96 Wadsworth Terrace, #5E
New York, NY 10040
212/795-0028

Meat & Potatoes Company
36 West 44th Street—Suite 1208
New York, NY 10036
718/403-0033
Herbert DuVal, Artistic Director

Medicine Show Theatre Ensemble
Box 20240
New York, NY 10025
212/431-9545
Barbara Vann, Artistic Director

Merely Players
P.O. Box 606
New York, NY 10108
212/799-2253

Merry Enterprises Theater
354 West 45th Street
New York, NY 10036
212/582-7862

Mirror Repertory Company
352 East 50th Street
New York, NY 10022
212/888-6087
Sabra Jones, Artistic Director

Modern Times Theatre
250 West 65th Street
New York, NY 10023
212/563-3292
Denny Partridge, Artistic Director

Musical Theatre Works
440 Lafayette Street
New York, NY 10003
212/677-0040
Anthony J. Stimac, Executive
Director; Mark S. Herko, Associate
Art Director

Music Theatre Group
735 Washington Street
New York, NY 10014
212/924-3108
Lyn Austin, Artistic Director

National Black Theatre
2033 Fifth Avenue
New York, NY 10035
212/427-5615
Tunde Samuel, Producer

National Improvisational Theatre
223 Eighth Avenue
New York, NY 10011
Tamara Wilcox, Artistic Director

Negro Ensemble Company
1560 Broadway—Suite 409
New York, NY 10036
212/575-5860
Leon Denmark, Producing
Director

New Federal Theatre
Henry Street Settlement
466 Grand Street
New York, NY 10002
212/598-0400
Woodie King, Jr., Artistic Director

New Rude Mechanicals
P.O. Box 2611
Times Square Station
New York, NY 10036
212/730-2030
Robert Hall, John Pynchon
Holmes: Artistic Directors

The New Stagecraft Co., Inc.
496A Hudson Street—Suite H-33
New York, NY 10014
212/757-6300 (service)
Daniel P. Quinn, Artistic Director

The New Theatre of Brooklyn
465 Dean Street
Brooklyn, NY 11217
718/768-5836

New York Gilbert & Sullivan
Players
251 West 91st Street, 4-C
New York, NY 10024
212/769-1000
Albert Bergeret, Artistic Director

New York Shakespeare Festival
425 Lafayette Street
New York, NY 10003
212/598-7100
Joseph Papp, Artistic
Director/Producer

New York Stage & Film Co.
John Housman Theater
450 West 42nd Street, #21
New York, NY 10036
212/967-3130
Leslie Urdang, Mark Linn-Baker,
Max Mayer: Producing Directors

New York Theatre Studio
130 West 80th Street
New York, NY 10024
802/388-3318
Joanna Gard, Artistic Director

New York Theatre Workshop
220 W. 42nd Street—18th Fl.
New York, NY 10036
212/302-7737
Nancy Kassak Diekmann,
Managing Director

On Stage Productions, Ltd.
50 West 97th Street, #8H
New York, NY 10025
212/666-1716
Lee Frank, Artistic Director

Ontological-Hysteric Theater
325 Spring Street—Suite 225
New York, NY 10013
212/243-6153
Richard Foreman, Artistic Director; George Ashley, Managing Director

The Open Eye: New Stagings
270 West 89th Street
New York, NY 10024
212/769-4141
Amie Brockway, Artistic Director

Open Space Theatre
P.O. Box 1018
Cooper Station
New York, NY 10003
212/254-8630
Lynn Michaels, Artistic Director

Pan Asian Repertory Theatre
47 Great Jones Street
New York, NY 10012
Tisa Chang, Artistic/Producing Director

Paper Bay Players
50 Riverside Drive
New York, NY 10024
212/362-0431
Judith Martin, Artistic Director

Pearl Theatre Company
125 West 22nd Street
New York, NY 10011
212/645-7708
Shepard Sobel, Artistic Director

Penguin Rep
1497 York Avenue
New York, NY 10021
212/650-9384
Dan Finnegan, Manager/Owner

Phoenix Ensemble
135 West 45th Street
New York, NY 10036
212/719-9148
Carter Inskeep, Artistic Director

Ping Chong & Company
253 Church Street
New York, NY 10013
212/966-0284
Ping Chong, Artistic Director

Playwrights Horizons
416 West 42nd Street
New York, NY 10036
212/564-1235
Andre Bishop, Artistic Director

Power Theatre Company
311 East 90th Street
New York, NY 10128
212/534-8390
Anthony DeRiso, Artistic Director

Primary Stages Company
584 Ninth Avenue
New York, NY 10036
212/333-7471
Casey Childs, Artistic Director

Project III Ensemble Theatre
P.O. Box 1502, Ansonia Station
New York, NY 10023
212/678-7526
Charles Otte, Artistic Director

Promethean Theatre
701 Seventh Avenue—Suite 9W
New York, NY 10036
212/719-9812
Dan Roentsch, Artistic Director

Prometheus Theatre
239 East 5th Street
New York, NY 10003
212/477-8689
Fred Fondren, Artistic Director

Puerto Rican Traveling Theatre
141 West 94th Street
New York, NY 10025
212/354-1293
Miriam Colon Valle, Artistic
Director

The Pyramid Group Theatre Co.
302 West 91st Street
New York, NY 10024
212/877-5166
Nico Hartos, Artistic Director

Quaigh Theatre
205 West 89th Street
New York, NY 10024
212/595-6185
Will Lieberson, Artistic Director

Quotidian Foundation
325 Spring Street—Suite 225
New York, NY 10013
212/243-6153
Stuart Sherman, Artistic Director;
Vincent Renzi, Business Manager

Rapp Theatre Company
220 East 4th Street
New York, NY 10009
212/529-5921
R. Jeffrey Cohen, Alexis S. Cohen:
Artistic Directors

The Real Theatre
140 West 69th Street, #11-1B
New York, NY 10023
212/724-3764; 994-0514
Jay Michaels, Artistic Director

Repertorio Espanol
Gramercy Arts Theater
138 East 27th Street
New York, NY 10016
212/889-2850
Rene Buch, Artistic Director;
Lilberto Zaldivar, Executive
Producer; Robert Weber Federico,
Resident Designer

The Restoration Proj. Theatre Co.
190 Washington Avenue
Brooklyn, NY 11205
718/624-0249
Felix Van Dijk, Artistic Director;
Rob Krakowski, Managing
Director

The Richard Allen Center for
Culture and Arts (RACCA)
550 West 155th Street
New York, NY 10032
212/281-2220
Shirley Radcliff, Producer

Ridiculous Theatrical Company
1 Sheridan Square
New York, NY 10014
212/691-2271
Everett Quinton, Artistic Director

Riverside Shakespeare Company
West-Park Presbyterian Church
165 West 86th Street
New York, NY 10024
212/877-6810
Tim Oman, Artistic Director

Riverwest Theatre
155 Bank Street
New York, NY 10014
212/243-0259
Nat Habib, Artistic Director

Roundabout Theatre Company
100 East 17th Street
New York, NY 10003
212/420-1360
Todd Haimes, Executive Director;
Gene Feist, Artistic Director

Royal Court Repertory
300 West 55th Street
New York, NY 10019
212/956-3500
Phillis Craig, Artistic Director

Ryan Repertory Company
2445 Bath Avenue
Brooklyn, NY 11214
718/373-5208
Barbara Parisi, Artistic Director;
John Sannuto, Acting Artistic
Director; Michelle Jacobs,
Managing Director

Sandcastle Players, Inc.
P.O. Box 1596
Cathedral Station
New York, NY 10025
212/677-6200
Jeanne Kaplan, Artistic Director

The Second Stage
P.O. Box 1807, Ansonia Station
New York, NY 10023
212/787-8302
Theatre address: 2162 Broadway,
New York, NY 10023
Robyn Goodman, Carole
Rothman: Artistic Directors;
Dorothy Maffei, Managing
Director

Second Story Ensemble
P.O. Box 21020
Columbus Circle Station
New York, NY 10023
212/957-9712
Janis Powell, Artistic Director

The Shaliko Company
151 2nd Avenue—Suite 1-E
New York, NY 10003
212/475-6313
Leonardo Shapiro, Artistic Dir.

Shelter West Company
440 West 42nd Street
New York, NY 10036-6805
Judith Joseph, Artistic Director

Roger Simon Studio
105 Llewellyn Road
Montclair, NJ 07042
212/JU6-6300 (service)
c/o Actors & Directors Lab, 412
West 42nd Street, New York, NY
10036
Roger Hendricks Simon, Artistic
Director

Soho Rep
80 Varick Street
New York, NY 10013
212/925-2588
Marlene Swartz, Jerry Engelbach:
Artistic Directors

Soupstone Project, Inc.
309 East 5th Street, #19
New York, NY 10003
212/473-7584
Neile Weissman, Artistic Director

South Street Theatre Co.
424 West 42nd Street
New York, NY 10036
212/564-0660
Jean Sullivan, Michael Fischetti:
Artistic Directors

Spectrum Theatre
1 East 104th Street, #9B
New York, NY 10029
212/475-5529
Benno Haehnel, Artistic Director

Spiderwoman Theatre
Workshop, Inc.
77 Seventh Avenue, #8S
New York, NY 10011
212/243-6209
Muriel Miguel, Artistic Director

Spuyten Duyvil
16 West 16th Street, #11FN
New York, NY 10011

Stage Left, Inc.
P.O. Box 3251
New York, NY 10185
212/989-4682
Patricia Vanderbeck, Artistic
Director

Staret...The Directors Co., Inc.
311 West 43rd Street—Suite 1404
New York, NY 10036
212/246-5877
Michael Parva, Artistic/Producing
Director

St. Bart's Playhouse
109 East 50th Street
New York, NY 10022
212/751-1616
Christopher Catt, Artistic Director

Thalia Spanish Theatre
P.O. Box 4368
Sunnyside, NY 11104
718/729-3880
Sylvia Brite, Artistic Director

Theatre For The New City
155-157 First Avenue
New York, NY 10003
212/254-1109
George Bartenieff, Crystal Field:
Artistic Directors

Theatre In Action
46 Walker Street
New York, NY 10013
212/431-1317
Lev Shekhtman, Artistic Director

Theatre Off Park
224 Waverly Place
New York, NY 10014
212/627-2556
Albert Harris, Artistic Director

Theatre 22
54 West 22nd Street
New York, NY 10011
212/243-2805
Sidney Armus, Sidney Salters:
Producers

Theatreworks/USA
890 Broadway
New York, NY 10003
212/677-5959
Jay Harnick, Artistic Director

Theco
99 Chrystie Street
New York, NY 10002
212/219-2450
Roberts Johnson, David Michael
Kronick: Co-Artistic Directors

Third Step Theatre Company
1179 Broadway
New York, NY 10001
212/545-1372
Al D'Andrea, Artistic Director;
Melody Brooks, Managing Director; Margit Ahlin, Literary Mgr

13th Street Theatre Repertory Co.
50 West 13th Street
New York, NY 10011
212/675-6677
Edith O'Hara, Terry Brogan:
Artistic Directors

TRG Repertory
c/o Marvin Kahan
60 East 8th Street
New York, NY 10003
212/757-6315
Marvin Kahan, Artistic Director

Triangle Theatre Co.
316 East 88th Street
New York, NY 10128
212/860-7245
Michael Remak, Molly O'Neil:
Artistic Directors

The Usual Suspects Theatre Co.
2819 West 12th Street, #9P
Brooklyn, NY 11224
718/946-4891
Robert Liebowitz, Director

Vietnam Veterans Ensemble
Theatre Company
c/o HBO
1100 Ave. of the Amer.—13th Fl.
New York, NY 10036
212/512-1960
Thomas Bird, Artistic Director

Village Players
103 Great Oaks Road
East Hill, NY 11577
516/621-0694
Gloria Poraino, Artistic Director

Village Theatre Company
Shandol Theater
137 West 22nd Street
New York, NY 10011
212/243-9504
Susan Farwell, Randy Kelly,
Marjorie Feenan, David
McConnell, Howard Thoresen:
Artistic Directors

The Vineyard Theatre
309 East 26th Street
New York, NY 10010
212/683-0696
Doug Aibel, Artistic Director

Vortex Theatre Company
164 Eleventh Avenue
New York, NY 10014
212/206-1764
Robert Coles, Artistic Director

Westbank Cafe
Downstairs Theater Bar
407 West 42nd Street
New York, NY 10036
212/695-6909
Rowan Joseph, Executive Director

Westbeth Theatre Center
151 Bank Street
New York, NY 10014
212/691-2272
Arnold Engelman, Producing
Director

Westside Community Repertory
Theatre
252 West 81st Street
New York, NY 10024
212/874-7290
Allen Schroeter, Artistic Director

The Willow Cabin Theatre Co.
10 Manhattan Avenue, #1E
New York, NY 10025
212/662-0077
Edward Berkeley, Artistic Director

Wings Theatre Company
521 City Island Avenue
Bronx, NY 10464
212/645-9630
Jeff Corrick, Artistic Director

Women's Project and Prod., Inc.
220 W. 42nd Street—18th Fl.
New York, NY 10036
212/382-2750
Julia Miles, Artistic Director

The Wooster Group
33 Wooster Street
New York, NY 10013
212/966-9796
Elizabeth Le Compte, Artistic
Director

Working Stages
316 West 93rd Street
New York, NY 10025
212/869-9770
Linda Laundra, Artistic Director

WPA Theatre
519 West 23rd Street
New York, NY 10011
212/206-0523
Kyle Renick, Artistic Director

York Theatre Company
2 East 90th Street
New York, NY 10028
212/534-5366
Janet Hayes Walker, Artistic
Director

The Yueh Lung Shadow Theatre
34-71 74th Street
Jackson Heights, NY 11372
718/478-6246
Jo Humphrey, Artistic Director

The following theaters may be used to house showcase productions by the various companies listed above and by other independent producers.

Actors' Outlet Theatre
120 West 28th Street
New York, NY 10001
212/807-1590

Judith Anderson Theatre
422 West 42nd Street
New York, NY 10036
212/736-7930

Harold Clurman Theatre
412 West 42nd Street
New York, NY 10036
212/594-2828

18th Street Playhouse
145 West 18th Street
New York, NY 10011
212/243-8643

Ernie Martin Studio Theatre
311 West 43rd Street
New York, NY 10036
212/397-5880

Sanford Meisner Theatre
164 11th Avenue
New York, NY 10011
212/206-1764

Perry Street Theatre
31 Perry Street
New York, NY 10014
212/255-7190

Chapter 15

Resident Theaters

The following is an up-to-date list of theaters operating under the Equity's League of Resident Theaters (LORT) contract. The names under the listings are those of the artistic and/or managing director(s).

ALABAMA

Alabama Shakespeare Festival
P.O. Box 20350
Montgomery, AL 36120-0350
205/272-1640
Martin Platt, James Volz

ARIZONA

Arizona Theater Company
56 West Congress—Box 1631
Tucson, AZ 85702
602/884-8210
Gary Gisselman, Susan Goldberg

CALIFORNIA

American Conservatory Theatre
450 Geary Street
San Francisco, CA 94102
415/771-3880
Edward Hastings, Diane Prichard

Berkeley Repertory Theater
2025 Addison Street
Berkeley, CA 94704
415/841-6108
Mitzi Sales, Sharon Ott

Berkeley Shakespeare Festival
Box 969, Berkeley, CA 94701
415/548-3422
Michael Addison, Susan Duncan

California Musical Theatre
30 N. Raymond Ave.—Suite 608
Pasadena, CA 91103
818/792-0776
Gary Davis

La Jolla Playhouse
P.O. Box 12039
La Jolla, CA 92037
619/452-6750
Des McAnuff, Alan Levey

L.A. Theater Center
514 South Spring Street
Los Angeles, CA 90013
213/627-6500
William Bushnell, Don Hill

Mark Taper Forum Los Angeles
Music Center
135 North Grand Avenue
Los Angeles, CA 90012
213/972-7384
Gordon Davidson, Steve Albert

Old Globe Theatre
P.O. Box 2171
San Diego, CA 92112
619/231-1941
Jack O'Brien, Thomas Hall

Pasadena Playhouse
39 South El Molino
Pasadena, CA 91101
818/792-8672
Susan Dietz, Lars Hansen

San Jose Repertory Company
Box 2399, San Jose, CA 95109-2399
408/294-7572
Timothy Near, Shannon Levak-
Leskin

Santa Barbara Theatre Festival
33 E. Canon Perdido Street
Santa Barbara, CA 93101
805/963-0761
Paul Blake, Esther Newitt

South Coast Repertory Theater
Box 2197
Costa Mesa, CA 92626
714/957-2602
David Emmes, Paula Tomei

COLORADO

Denver Center Theatre Company
1050 13th Street
Denver, CO 80204
303/893-4200
Donovan Marley, Sarah Lawless

CONNECTICUT

Goodspeed Opera House East
Haddam, CT 06423
203/873-8664
Michael Price, Sue Frost

Hartford Stage Company
50 Church Street
Hartford, CT 06103
203/525-5601
Mark Lamos, David Hawkanson

Long Wharf Theatre
222 Sargent Drive
New Haven, CT 06511
203/787-4284
Arvin Brown, M. Edgar Rosen-
blum

Eugene O'Neill Memorial Theatre
National Playwrights Conf.
305 Great Neck Road
Waterford, CT 06385
203/443-5378
Lloyd Richards

Yale Repertory Theatre
Yale School of Drama
222 York Street
New Haven, CT 06520
203/432-1515
Lloyd Richards, Benjamin
Mordecai

DISTRICT OF COLUMBIA

Arena Stage
6th & Main Avenue SW
Washington, DC 20024
202/554-9066
Zelda Fichandler, William Stewart

Folger Theatre Group
201 E. Capitol Street SE
Washington, DC 20003
202/547-3230
Michael Kahn, Mary Ann
DiBarbieri

FLORIDA

Asolo Theatre Festival
P.O. Box Drawer E
Sarasota, FL 33578
813/355-7115
John Ulmer, Donna Gerdes

Caldwell Theatre Company
P.O. Box 277
Boca Raton, FL 33432
305/368-7509
Michael Hall

Coconut Grove Playhouse
P.O. Box 616, Miami, FL 33133
305/442-2662
Arnold Mittelman, Jordan Black

The Hippodrome State Theatre
25 Southeast 2nd Place
Gainesville, FL 32601
904/373-5968
Mary Hausch, David Black

GEORGIA

Alliance Theatre Company
1280 Peachtree Street NE
Atlanta, GA 30309
404/898-1119
Robert Farley, Edith Love

ILLINOIS

Goodman Theatre Company
200 South Columbus Drive
Chicago, IL 60603
312/443-3811
Robert Falls, Roche Schulfer

The North Light Repertory
Theatre, Inc.
2300 Green Bay Road
Evanston, IL 60201
312/869-7732
Russell Vandenbrouchke, Susan
Medak

INDIANA

Indiana Repertory Theatre
140 West Washington Street
Indianapolis, IN 46204
317/635-5266
Tom Haas, Victoria Nolan

KENTUCKY

Actors Theatre of Louisville
316-320 West Main Street
Louisville, KY 40202
502/584-1265
Jon Jory, Alexander Speer

MAINE

Portland Stage Company
P.O. Box 1458
Portland, ME 04104
207/774-1043
Barbara Rosoff, Mark Somers

MARYLAND

Center Stage
700 North Calvert Street
Baltimore, MD 21202
301/685-3200
Stan Wojewodski, Peter Culman

MASSACHUSETTS

American Repertory Theatre Co.
Loeb Drama Center
64 Brattle Street
Cambridge, MA 02138
617/495-2668
Robert Brustein, Robert Orchard

Berkshire Theatre Festival
Main Street
Stockbridge, MA 01262
413/298-5536
Richard Dunlop, Carol Dougherty

Huntington Theatre Company
Boston University Theater
264 Huntington Avenue
Boxton, MA 02115
617/353-3320
Peter Altman, Michael Maso

Merrimack Regional Theatre
P.O. Box 228
Lowell, MA 01853
508/454-6324
Daniel Schay

Shakespeare & Company/Boston
Shakespeare
52 Saint Botolph Street
Boston, MA 02116
617/267-5630
Tina Packer, Dennis Krusnick

Shakespeare & Co./The Mount
Lenox, MA 01240
412/637-1197
Tina Packer, Dennis Krusnick

Stagewest
Springfield Theatre Arts Assoc.
1 Columbus Center
Springfield, MA 01103
413/781-4470
Gregory Boyd, Val Pori

MICHIGAN

Actors Theatre of St. Paul
28 West 7 Place
Saint Paul, MN 55102
612/297-6868
Michael Andrew Miner, Martha
Richards

Meadow Brook Theatre
Oakland University
Rochester, MI 48063
313/377-3300
Terence Kilburn, James Spittle

MISSOURI

Missouri Repertory Theatre
Univ. of MO at Kansas City
5100 Rockhill Road
Kansas City, MO 64110
816/363-4300
George Keathley, Robert Thatch

The Repertory Theatre of St. Louis
130 Edgar Road
Saint Louis, MO 63119
314/968-7342
Mark Bernstein, Steven Woolf

NEW HAMPSHIRE

American Stage Festival
P.O. Box 225
Milford, NH 03005
603/673-4005
Larry Carpenter,
Richard Rose

NEW JERSEY

George St. Playhouse
9 Livingston Avenue
New Brunswick, NJ 08901
201/846-2895
Gregory Hurst, Michael Gennaro

McCarter Theatre Company, Inc.
Princeton University
91 University Place
Princeton, NJ 08540
609/683-9100
Nagle Jackson, John Herochik

N.J. Shakespeare Festival
Science Hall
Drew University,
Route 24
Madison, NJ 07940
201/377-5330
Paul Barry, Richard Yarnell

The Whole Theatre Company
544 Bloomfield Avenue
Montclair, NJ 07042
201/744-2996
Olympia Dukakis, Scott Clugstone

NEW MEXICO

New Mexico Repertory Theatre
P.O. Box 789
Albuquerque, NM 87103
505/243-4577
Andrew Shea, John Beauchamps

NEW YORK

Acting Company Touring
420 W. 42nd Street—3rd Floor
New York, NY 10036
212/564-3510
Margot Harley, Mary Beth Carroll

Capital Repertory Company
P.O. Box 399 Albany, NY 12201
518/462-4531
Peter Clough, Bruce Bouchard

Circle In The Square
1633 Broadway
New York, NY 10019
212/307-2700
Theodore Mann, Paul Libin

Geva Theatre
75 Woodbury Blvd.
Rochester, NY 14605
716/232-1366
Howard Milman, Thomas Pechar

Lincoln Center Theatre Company
165 West 65th Street
New York, NY 10023
212/362-7600
Gregory Mosher, Steve Callahan

Long Island Stage
Box 9001, Rockville Ctr, NY 11571
516/546-4600
Clint Atkinson

Negro Ensemble Company
165 West 46th Street
New York, NY 10036
212/575-5860
Douglas Turner Ward, Leon
Denmark

NY Shakespeare Festival
The Public Theater
425 Lafayette Street
New York, NY 10003
212/598-7100
Joseph Papp, Bob MacDonald

Roundabout Theatre Company
100 East 17th Street
New York, NY 10003
212/420-1360
Gene Feist, Todd Haimes

Studio Arena Theatre
710 Maine Street
Buffalo, NY 14202
716/856-8025
David Frank, Raymond Bonnard

Syracuse Stage
John D. Archbold Theater
820 East Genesee Street
Syracuse, NY 13210
315/423-4008
Arthur Storch, James A. Clark

NORTH CAROLINA

Charlotte Repertory Theatre
Spirit Square, 110 East 7th Street
Charlotte, NC 28202
704/375-4796
Mark Woods, Keith Stevens

North Carolina Shakespeare
Festival
P.O. Box 6066
High Point, NC 27262
919/841-6273
Lou Rackoff, Pedro Silva

Playmakers Repertory Company
206 Graham Memorial 052A
Chapel Hill, NC 27514
919/962-1122
Margaret Hahn, David Hammond

OHIO

Cincinnati Playhouse In The Park
P.O. Box 6537
Cincinnati, OH 45206
513/421-5440
Worth Gardner, Kathleen Panoff

Cleveland Play House
Box 1989
Cleveland, OH 44106
216/795-7010
Josephine Abady, Dean Gladden

Great Lakes Theater Festival
1501 Euclid Avenue—Suite 250
Cleveland, OH 44115
216/241-5490
Gerald Fredman, Mary Bill

PENNSYLVANIA

Gretna Productions, Inc.
P.O. Box 578
Mt. Gretna, PA 17064
717/964-3627
Paul Giovanni, Trish Rasmus

Pennsylvania Stage Company
J.I. Rodale Theater
837 Linden Street
Allentown, PA 18101
215/434-6110
Peter Wrenn-Meleck, Rosalie
Schreiber

People's Light & Theatre Co.
39 Conestoga Road
Malvern, PA 19355
215/647-1900
Danny Fruchter, Gregory T.
Rowe

Philadelphia Drama Guild
112 16th Street—Suite 802
Philadelphia, PA 19102
215/563-7530
Gregory Poggi, Kathleen Nolan

Philadelphia Festival Theatre For
New Plays
3900 Chestnut Street
Philadelphia, PA 10104-3105
212/222-5000
Carol Rocamora, Grace Grillet

Pittsburgh Public Theatre
Allegheny Square
Pittsburgh, PA 15212-5362
412/323-8200
William Gardner, Dan Fallon

Walnut Street Theatre
9th & Walnut Streets
Philadelphia, PA 19107
215/574-3550
Bernard Havard, Lynn Fitzpatrick

RHODE ISLAND

Trinity Square Repertory Co.
201 Washington Street
Providence, RI 02903
401/521-1100
Adrian Hall, E. Timothy Langan

TENNESSEE

Clarence Brown Theatre
P.O. Box 8450
Knoxville, TN 37996
615/974-3447
Thomas P. Cooke, Kevin Coleman

Tennessee Rep.
427 Chestnut Street
Nashville, TN 37203
615/244-4878
Mac Pirkle, Brian Laczko

TEXAS

Alley Theatre
615 Texas Avenue
Houston, TX 77002
713/228-9341
Jim Bernhard, Chris Kawolsky

Dallas Theatre Center
3636 Turtle Creek Blvd.
Dallas, TX 75219
214/526-5671
Adrian Hall, Peter Connelly

Paramount Theatre
P.O. Box 1205
Austin, TX 78767
512/474-2901
Linda Hansen

Plaza Theatre
2914 Greenville Avenue
Dallas, TX 75206
214/823-3670
Lou Moore

Theatre Three
2800 Routh Street
Dallas, TX 75201
214/651-7225
Jac Alder, Peggy Kincade

UTAH

Pioneer Memorial Theatre
University of Utah
Salt Lake City, UT 84112
810/581-6206
Charles Morey

VIRGINIA

Barter Theatre
Box 867
Abingdon, VA 24210
703/628-2281
Red Partington

Theatre Virginia
Boulevard & Grove Avenues
Richmond, VA 23221
804/257-0840
Terry Burgler

Virginia Stage Company
P.O. Box 3770, 254 Granby Street
Norfolk, VA 23514
804/627-6988
Charles Towers, Dan Martin

WASHINGTON

A Contemporary Theatre
100 West Roy St.—Box 19400
Seattle, WA 98119
206/285-3220
Jeff Steitzer, Phil Schermer

Intiman Theatre Company
P.O. Box 19645
Seattle, WA 98109
206/624-4541
Elizabeth Huddle, Peter Davis

Seattle Repertory Theatre
Bagley Wright Theater
155 Mercer Street
Seattle, WA 98109
206/447-2210
Daniel Sullivan, Ben Moore

WISCONSIN

Milwaukee Repertory Theatre Co.
108 East Wells Street
Milwaukee, WI 53202
414/224-1761
John Dillon, Sara O'Connor

Chapter 16

Equity Dinner Theaters

In this chapter and the next, the names listed after each theater are those of the owner(s) and/or producer(s).

The designations ADTI and NDTA indicate membership in one of the two national dinner theater organizations: the American Dinner Theatre Institute (ADTI) which is almost exclusively Equity; or the National Dinner Theatre Institute (NDTA) which is exclusively non-Equity.

CALIFORNIA

The Grand Dinner Theatre
Grand Hotel
One Hotel Way
Anaheim, CA 92802
714/772-7710 or 772-3220
Frank Syka
ADTI

Harlequin Dinner Playhouse
3503 South Harbor Blvd.
Santa Ana, CA 92704
714/979-7550
Al & Barbara Hampton

Lawrence Welk Village Theatre
8975 Lawrence Welk Drive
Escondido, CA 92026
Robert M. Dias   (ADTI)

COLORADO

Country Dinner Playhouse
6875 South Clinton
Englewood, CO 80110
303/771/1410 or 771-9311
Bill McHale, Producer
ADTI
All correspondence to:
P.O Box 3167
Englewood, CO 80155

CONNECTICUT

Coachlight Dinner Theatre
266 Main Street
East Windsor, CT 06088
203/623-8227 or 623-2021
Janis Belkin
ADTI

Darien Dinner Theatre
65 Tokeneke Road
Darien, CT 06820
203/655-6812 or 838-8411
Jane Bergere
ADTI

FLORIDA

Alhambra Dinner Theatre
1200 Beach Blvd.
Jacksonville, FL 32216
904/641-1212
Tod Booth, Executive Producer
ADTI

Burt Reynolds Dinner Theatre
1001 East Indiantown Road
Jupiter, FL 33458
407/747-5261 or 746-5566
Karen Poindexter, Producer
ADTI

Golden Apple Dinner Theatre
25 North Pineapple Avenue
Sarasota, FL 33577
813/366-3646 or 5454 (box off.)
Robert E. Turoff
ADTI

The Hirschfeld Theatre
The Castle Hotel & Resort
5445 Collins Avenue
Miami Beach, FL 33140
305/866-0014
Karen Poindexter
ADTI

Mark II Dinner Theatre
3376 Edgewater Drive
Orlando, FL 32804-3797
407/843-6275
Mark Howard
ADTI/NDTA

Royal Palm Dinner Theatre
303 Golf View Drive
Royal Palm Plaza
Boca Raton, FL 33432
407/392-3755
Jan McArt
ADTI

Showboat Dinner Theatre
3405 Ulmerton Road
P.O. Box 519
Clearwater, FL 33520
813/576-3818 or 223-2545
Maurice Shinners
ADTI

ILLINOIS

Candlelight Dinner Playhouse
5620 South Harlem Avenue
Summit, IL 60501
312/735-7400 or 496-3000
William Pulinsi
ADTI

Drury Lane Oakbrook Theatre
100 Drury Lane
Oakbrook Terrace, IL 60181
312/530-8300
Tony De Santis
ADTI

Drury Lane South
2500 West Drury Lane
Evergreen Park, IL 60642
312/779-4000
John Lazzara

Mariott's Lincolnshire Theatre
101 Half Day Road
Lincolnshire, IL 60015
Kary M. Walker
ADTI

INDIANA

Beef 'N' Boards Dinner Theatre
9301 North Michigan Road
Indianapolis, IN 46268
317/872-9664
Doug Stark, Robert Zehr
ADTI/NDTA

MINNESOTA

Chanhassen Dinner Theatre
P.O Box 99
Chanhassen, MN 55317
612/934-1500 or 934-1525
Richard Bloomberg
ADTI

Chanhassen Playhouse Dinner
Theatre
Chanhassen, MN 55317
612/934-1500 or 934-1525
Richard Bloomberg
ADTI

Fireside Dinner Theatre
51 West 78th Street
Chanhassen, MN 55317
612/934-1500
Richard Bloomberg
ADTI
All correspondence to:
P.O. Box 99
Chanhassen, MN 55317

MISSOURI

Tiffany's Attic Dinner Theatre
5208 Main Street
Kansas City, MO 64112
816/361-2661 or 561-7923
Dennis Hennesy
ADTI

Waldorf Astoria Dinner Playhouse
7428 Washington
Kansas City, MO 64112
816/561-7921 or 561-1704
Dennis Hennessy
ADTI
All correspondence to:
5028 Main Street
Kansas City, MO 64112
816/361-2661

NEBRASKA

Firehouse Dinner Theatre
514 South 11th Street
Omaha, NE 68102
402/346-6009 or 346-8833
Richard Mueller   (ADTI/NDTA)

NEW YORK

An Evening Dinner Theatre
11 Clearbrook Road
Elmsford, NY 10523
914/592-2268 or 592-2222
William Stutler, Robert Funking
ADTI

Lake George Dinner Theatre
P.O. Box 266
Lake George, NY 12845
518/668-1258
David Eastwood   (ADTI)

OHIO

Carousel Dinner Theatre
1275 East Waterloo Road
Akron, OH 44306
216/724-9855
Scott Griffith   (ADTI)
All correspondence to:
P.O. Box 7530
Akron, OH 44306

Westgate Dinner Theatre
3301 West Central Avenue
P.O. Box 2988
Toledo, OH 43606
419/537-1881
Ken Shaw

TEXAS

Country Squire Dinner Theatre
135 Sunset Market Town
Amarillo, TX 79120
806/358-7486
Peter Fox, Della Ray

Dinner Theater
Associations

American Dinner Theatre Institute
Box 367
Cockeysville, MD 21030
Joshua Cockey, Exec. Director

National Dinner Theatre
Association
58 North Ambler Street
Quakertown, PA 18951
212/538-3206
Richard Akins, Chairman

Chapter 17

Non-Equity Dinner Theaters

ALABAMA

Blue Moon Dinner Theatre
1447 Montgomery Highway
Birmingham, AL 35216
205/823-3000
Judith Peacock, Bob King (NDTA)

ARKANSAS

Murry's Dinner Theatre
6323 Asher Avenue
Little Rock, AK 72204
501/562-3131
Ike Murray   (ADTI/NDTA)

CALIFORNIA

Firelite Dinner Theatre
4350 Transport Street
Ventura, CA 93003
805/656-3922
Kathryn Taylor   (ADTI)

Roger Rocka's Music Hall
1266 North Wishon
Fresno, CA 93728
209/266-9493
Roger Rocka   (ADTI)

COLORADO

Heritage Square Music Hall
5 Heritage Square
Golden, CO 80401
303/279-7800
Woddy Wirth

DELAWARE

Candlelight Music Dinner Theatre
2208 Miller Road
Ardentown, DE 19810
302 475-2313
John O'Toole

All correspondence to:
P.O. Box 7301
Wilmington, DE 19803

FLORIDA

Country Dinner Playhouse
7951 Gateway Mall
9th Street North
St. Petersburg, FL 33702
813/577-5515
David Gardner
NDTA

Marco Polo Dinner Theatre
19201 Collins Avenue
N. Miami Beach, FL 33160
305/932-2233

Naples Dinner Theatre
1025 Piper Blvd.
Naples, FL 33942
813/597-6031
Jules Fiske, Jim Fargo
NDTA

ILLINOIS

Circa '21 Dinner Playhouse
P.O. Box 3784
1828 Third Avenue
Rock Island, IL 61201
309/785-2667
Dennis Hitchcock
NDTA

Conklin Players Dinner Theatre
P.O. Box 301
Conklin Court
Goodfield, IL 61742
309/965-2545
In Illinois: 800-322-2304
Chaunce Conklin
ADTI/NDTA

Sunshine Dinner Theatre
115 West Kirby Avenue
Champaign, IL 61820
217/359-4503
Arthur L. Barnes   (NDTA)

INDIANA

Derby Dinner Theatre
525 Marriott Drive
Clarksville, IN 47130
812/288-2634
Bekki Jo Schneider
NDTA

IOWA

Ingersoll Dinner Theatre
3711 Ingersoll Avenue
Des Moines, IA 50312
515/274-4686
Charles Carnes
ADTI/NDTA

KANSAS

Crown Uptown Dinner Theatre
3207 East Douglas
Wichita, KS 67218
316/681-1566
Karen & Ted Morris
NDTA

MARYLAND

Burne Brae Dinner Theatre
Route 29
Burtonville, MD 20866
301/384-5800
John Kinnamon
NDTA

Harborlights Dinner Theatre
511 South Broadway
Baltimore, MD 21231
301/522-4126
F. Scott Black   (ADTA)

Harlequin Dinner Theatre
1330 East Gude Drive
Rockville, MD 20850
301/340-6813
Nicholas Howey, Kenneth Gentry
NDTA

Petrucci's Dinner Theatre
312 Main Street
Laurel, MD 20707
301/725-5226
C. David Petrucci

Towson Towne Musical
Dinner Theatre
7800 York Road
Towson, MD 21204
301/321-6595
F. Scott Black

MICHIGAN

Cornwell's Turkeyville
Dinner Theatre
18935 15 Mile Road
Marshall, MI 49068
616/781-7933 or 781-4315
David M. Pritchard
ADTI/NDTA
All correspondence to:
Pritchard Productions
P.O. Box 734
Marshall, MI 49127

Schuler's Stevensville
Dinner Theatre
5000 Red Arrow Highway
Stevensville, MI 49127
616/781-7933
David M. Pritchard
ADTI/NDTA
All correspondence to:
Pritchard Productions
P.O. Box 734
Marshall, MI 49127

MISSOURI

Goldenrod Showboat
700 N. L.K. Sullivan Blvd.
St. Louis, MO 63102
314/621-3311
Frank Pierson   (ADTI/NDTA)

NEBRASKA

Upstairs Dinner Theatre
221 South 19th Street
Omaha, NE 68102
402/344-3858
Anne Ausdemore   (NDTA)

NEW JERSEY

Neil's New Yorker Dinner Theatre
Rt. 46 Mountain Lakes, NJ 07046
201/334-0010
Jack Bell   (NDTA)

NEW YORK

Island Squire Dinner Theatre
P.O. Box 428
Middle Island, NY 19953
516/732-2240
John Wyle

NORTH CAROLINA

The Barn
120 Stage Coach Trail
Greensboro, NC 27409
919/292-2211
Thomas F. Hennis, Jr.   (NDTA)

OHIO

La Comedia Dinner Theatre
P.O. Box 204
Springboro, OH 45066
513/746-3114
Ed Flesch   (NDTA)

PENNSYLVANIA

Allenberry Playhouse
P.O. Box 7—Route 174
Boiling Springs, PA 17007
717/258-6120
John Heinze
NDTA

Dutch Apple Dinner Theatre
510 Centerville Road
Lancaster, PA 17601
717/898-1900
Prather Productions
ADTI/NDTA

Genetti Dinner Playhouse
Route 309
Hazelton, PA 18201
717/455-3691
Richard Akins Productions
NDTA

Huntingdon Valley
Dinner Theatre
2633 Philmont Avenue
Huntingdon Valley, PA 19006
215/947-6000

Peddler's Village Dinner Theatre
Route 263
Lahaska, PA 18931
215/794-3460
NDTA

VIRGINIA

Barksdale Dinner Theatre
P.O. Box 7
Hanover, VA 23069
804/537-5333
Nancy Kilgore

Barn Dinner Theatre
Salem, VA
703/387-2276
Mary Gilchrift

Swift Creek Mill Playhouse
P.O. Box 41
Colonial Heights, VA 23834
804/748-5203
Wamer J. Callahan

Tidewater Dinner Theatre
6270 Northampton Blvd.
Norfolk, VA 23502
804/461-2933
Maureen J. Sigmund
ADTI/NDTA

WISCONSIN

Fanny Hill Supper Club and
Dinner Theatre
Route 5
Eau Claire, WI 54701
715/836-8184

Fireside Playhouse
1131 Janesville Avenue
Ft. Atkinson, WI 53538
414/563-9505
E. Flesch
NDTA

Northern Lights Playhouse &
Pinewood Dinner Theatre
P.O. Box 256
Hazelhurst, WI 54531
715/356-7173
Michael D. Cupp
NDTA

Chapter 18

Industrial Show Production Companies

Armstrong World Industries
150 North Queen Street
Lancaster, PA 17603
717/397-0611 or 396-4203
Fred A. Stoner

Avion Communications
230 West 17th Street
New York, NY 10011
212/807-0044
Julie Sasvari

Gene Bayliss
16 Burritts Landing
Westport, CT 06880
203/227-7521

Big Brothers & Big Sisters Inc.
324 East Wisconsin—Suite 543
Milwaukee, WI 53202
414/278-7764
Margaret Lange-Lewis

Bolduc & Bradley
950 Third Avenue—25th Floor
New York, NY 10022
212/832-7700
Bill Mayhew

Michael Brown Enterprises, Inc.
335 East 50th Street
New York, NY 10022
212/759-2233
Michael Brown

Caribiner, Inc.
16 West 61st Street
New York, NY 10023
212/541-5809
Mike Meth

Michael Carson Productions
250 West 54th Street
New York, NY 10019-5515
212/765-2300
Michael Carson

The Chartmakers Inc.
33 West 60th Street
New York, NY 10023
212/247-7200
Steve Reiter

Comart Aniforms, Inc.
360 West 31st Street
New York, NY 10001
212/714-2550
Gary Saltzer

Concepts Unlimited
315 West 57th Street
New York, NY 10019
212/246-9612
Richard Barclay

Contempo Communications
251 West 19th Street—Suite 10D
New York, NY 10011
212/633-2333
Joan Marshall

Corporate Concepts, Ltd.
260 Fifth Avenue
New York, NY 10001
212/545-0933
Jack Schatz, President

Creative Presentations
819 West Lunt Avenue
Shaumburg, IL 60193
312/894-2248
Gene Bullard

CTP Casting
22 West 27th Street—10th Floor
New York, NY 10001
212/696-1100
Lisbeth Andersen

Decomas Inc.
441 Lexington Avenue
New York, NY 10017
212/953-9030
Judith M. Little, Sondra Arnold

Frank Egan & Associates
c/o Leo Burnett Co., Inc.
26555 Evergreen Road
Southfield, MI 48076
313/355-1900
or: Leo Burnett Co., Inc.
950 Third Ave., NY, NY 10022

Imero Fiorentino Assoc.
44 West 63rd Street
New York, NY 10023
212/246-0600
Corky Thueson

Fourmost Productions, Inc.
60 Idaho Street
Passaic Park, NJ 07055
201/777-8357
Paul Kastl

Gindick Productions
21 East 40th Street, PH
New York, NY 10016
212/725-2580
J. Jeff Salmon

Goodsight/Herrmann
850 7th Avenue—Suite 1200
New York, NY 10019
Larry Goodsight

Graphic Media Communications
373 Route 46 West
Fairfield, NJ 07006
201/227-5000
Julie Charles

Heller Creative Inc.
14 Foothill Street
Putnam Valley, NY 10579
914/528-6328
Buck Heller

Michael John Associates, Inc.
39 Lewis Street
Greenwich, CT 06830
203/622-0777
R.M. Duffy, Chairman

George P. Johnson Company
800 Techrow
Madison Heights, MI 48071
Robert Vallee, Owner; Ron Williams, VP & National Dir. of Sales

Maritz Communications Co.
1515 Route 10
Parsippany, NJ 07054
201/540-1761

Marketing Concepts, Inc.
1500 Broadway—Suite 2304
New York, NY 10036
212/382-0171
Neva Conley

Medical Multi Media Corp.
211 East 43rd Street—Suite 2302
New York, NY 10017
Stanley Waine

Meeting Environments
9 East 19th Street
New York, NY 10003
212/677-3500
Joe Iorio, Doug Speer

Metropolitan Life Insurance
1 Madison Avenue
New York, NY 10010
212/578-8715
Beth Dembitzer

Jack Morton Productions, Inc.
830 Third Avenue
New York, NY 10022
212/758-8400
Bill Morton, President

Motivation Media, Inc.
1245 Milwaukee Avenue
Glenview, IL 60025
312/297-4740
Glen Peterson, Production
Manager

National Speakers Bureau
222 Wisconsin Avenue
Lake Forest, IL 60045
312/295-1122
John Palmer, President

Pepsi Cola Company
P.O. Box 442
Somers, NY 10589
914/767-6000
Patrik J. Williams

Radio City Music Hall Productions
1260 Avenue of the Americas
New York, NY 10020
212/246-4600
Winnie Boone

Sandy Corporation
1500 West Big Beaver Road
Troy, MI 48084
313/649-0800

Second Sight Inc.
Basking Ridge, NJ 07920
201/822-4684
Benjamin Evans

Sheridan Jennings, Ltd.
155 North Harbor Drive
Concourse Level
Chicago, IL 60601
312/565-0002
Joseph T. Jennings, President

Phoebe Snow Productions
37 West 36th Street
New York, NY 10018
212/679-8756
Deborah Herr

Sorgel Studios, Inc.
205 West Highland Avenue
Milwaukee, WI 53203
414/224-9600
James K. Henley, Producer &
Director

Trajectory
140 Riverside Drive
New York, NY 10024
212/724-2200
Don Doherty

Visual Services & Intergroup
Productions
1 West 19th Street
New York, NY 10011
212/580-9551

John R. Walsh & Associates
450 Seventh Avenue
New York, NY 10123
212/753-9800
John R. Walsh

Weiss-Watson
1140 Avenue of the Americas
New York, NY 10036
212/753-9800
Sal Rasa

Zacks & Perrier
96 Morton Street
New York, NY 10014
212/463-7308
Duane Butler

Chapter 19

Theme Park Show Producers

The names given are, in most cases, the entertainment coordinators at the parks.

Action Park
P.O. Box 848
McAfee, NJ 07428

Allan Albert, Inc.
561 Broadway—Suite 10C
New York, NY 10012
212/966-8881

Astroworld
9001 Kirby Drive
Houston, TX 77054
713/799-8404
Michael Svatek

Boardwalk and Baseball
P.O. Box 800
Orlando, FL 32802
305/648-5151, ext. 7222
Bob LaPratt

Busch Gardens—The Dark
Continent
P.O. Box 9158
Tampa, FL 33674-9158
813/988-5171
Doug Braconnier

Busch Gardens—The Old Country
P.O. Drawer F.C.
Williamsburg, VA 23186
804/253-3300
Linda Cuddihy

Cedar Point/The Amazement Park
C.N. 5006
Cypress Gardens, FL 33884
305/351-5901
Steven DeWoody

Disneyland
1313 Harbor Blvd.
Anaheim, CA 92803
714/490-3125 or 999-4000
Dave Goodman

Dollywood
700 Dollywood Lane
Pigeon Forge, TN 37863-4101
615/428-9433
Michael Padgett

Hersheypark
100 West Hersheypark Drive
Hershey, PA 17033
717/534-3349
Bonnie Bosso

Kings Productions
1932 Highland Avenue
Cincinnati, OH 45219
513/241-8989
Dan Schultz

Opryland
2802 Opryland Drive
Nashville, TN 37214
615/871-6656
Susan Bablove

Sea World of Florida
6277 Sea Harbor Drive
Orlando, FL 32887
305/345-5168
Entertainment Department

Sea World of Ohio
1100 Sea World Drive
P.O. Box 237, Aurora, OH 44202
216/562-8101
Entertainment Office

Sea World of San Diego
1720 South Shores Road
Mission Bay, San Diego, CA 92109
619/222-6363
Entertainment Department

Sea World of Texas
2548 Boardwalk
San Antonio, TX 78217
512/523-3000
Henry Hartman

Sesame Place
100 Sesame Road
Langhorne, PA 19067
215/752-7070
Greg Hartley

Show Biz International, Inc.
5142 Old Boonville Highway
Evansville, IN 47715
812/473-0880
Maria A. Rivers

Six Flags Corporation Show
Productions
1168 113th Street
Grand Prairie, TX 75050
214/988-8332

Six Flags Great Adventure
P.O. Box 120
Jackson, NJ 08527
201/928-2200
Show Operations

Six Flags Great America
P.O. Box 1776
Gurnee, IL 60031
312/249-1776, Ext. 4650
David Carter

Six Flags Magic Mountain
P.O. Box 5500
Valencia, CA 91355
805/255-4858
Show Operations

Six Flags Over Georgia
P.O. Box 43187
Atlanta, GA 30378
404/948-9290
Show Operations

Six Flags Over Mid-America
P.O. Box 666
Eureka, MO 63025
314/938-5300
Show Operations

Six Flags Over Texas
P.O. Box 191
Arlington, TX 76004
817/640-8900
Show Operations

Walt Disney World
P.O. Box 10,000
Lake Buena Vista, FL 32830
305/345-5745
Larry Smith

Walt Disney World/Epcot Institute
P.O. Box 10,000
Lake Buena Vista, FL 32830
305/345-5755
Bob Radock

Worlds of Fun
4545 Worlds of Fun Avenue
Kansas City, MO 64161
816/454-4545
Gary Noble

Chapter 20

Industry Unions

Screen Actors Guild (SAG) Offices

National Headquarters
7065 Hollywood Blvd.
Hollywood, CA 90028
213/465-4600

5150 North 16th Street, #C-255
Phoenix, AZ 85016
602/279-9975

3045 Rosecrans Avenue, #308
San Diego, CA 94104
619/222-3996

100 Bush Street
San Francisco, CA 94104
415/391-7510

950 South Cherry Street, #502
Denver, CO 80222
303/757-6226

145 Madeira Avenue
Coral Gables, FL 33134
305/444-7677

2299 Douglas Road, Ste. West
Miami, FL 33145
305/444-7677

1627 Peachtree Street N.E., #210
Atlanta, GA 30309
404/897-1335

949 Kapiolani Blvd., #105
Honolulu, HI 96814
808/538-6122

307 North Michigan
Chicago, IL 60601
312/372-8081

The Highland House
5480 Wisconsin Avenue, #201
Chevy Chase, MD 20815
301/657-2560

11 Beacon Street, #512
Boston, MA 02108
617/742-2688

28690 Southfield Road
Lathrup Village, MI 48076
313/559-9540

15 South Ninth Street, #400
Minneapolis, MN 55404
612/371-9120

906 Olive Street, #1006
St. Louis, MO 63101
619/231-8410

1515 Broadway—44th Floor
New York, NY 10036
212/944-1030

1367 East Sixth Street, #229
Cleveland, OH 44114
216/579-9305

230 S. Broad Street—10th Floor
Philadelphia, PA 19102
215/545-3150

1108 17th Avenue South
Nashville, TN 37212
615/327-2958

2650 Fountainview
Houston, TX 77057
713/972-1806

6309 North O'Connor Road
Irving, TX 75039
214/869-3556

601 Valley Street, #200
Seattle, WA 98109
206/282-2506

American Federation Of Television And Radio Artists (AFTRA)

6922 Hollywood Blvd.
Hollywood, CA 90078
213/461-8111

100 Bush Street
San Francisco, CA 94104
415/391-7510

20401 NW Second Avenue
Miami, FL 33169
305/652-4824

307 North Michigan
Chicago, IL 60601
312/372-8081

24901 Northwestern Highway
Southfield, MI 48075
313/354-1774

260 Madison Avenue
New York, NY 10016
212/532-0800

2650 Fountainview
Houston, TX 77057
713/972-1806

6309 North O'Connor Road
Irving, TX 75039
214/869-3556

Actors Equity Association (AEA)

6430 West Sunset Blvd.
Los Angeles, CA 90028
213/462-2334

100 Bush Street
San Francisco, CA 94104
415/391-7510

203 North Wabash
Chicago, IL 60601
312/641-0393

165 West 46th Street
New York, NY 10036
212/869-8530

Chapter 21

Industry Publications

BACK STAGE
P.O. Box 2078
Mahopac, NY 10541

Weekly; $50.00/yr.

MADISON AVENUE
HANDBOOK

An annual directory for the advertising and communications industries featuring 24 tabbed sections
including Media; Production; Professional Services; Music & Sound;
Film Commissions; Equipment,
Studios & Stages; Model and Talent Agencies, and more...$45.00.

ROSS REPORTS TELEVISION
Television Index, Inc.
40-29 27th Street
Long Island City, NY 11101

Monthly publication listing advertising agencies, casting directors,
and franchised agents in the New
York area.

Subscriptions: $17.00/6 mos;
$32.00/1yr.

SHOW BUSINESS
1501 Broadway
New York, NY 10036

Weekly; $40.00/1 yr; $65.00/2 yrs.

Chapter 22

Some Final Thoughts

Writing this book has given me a tremendous amount of satisfaction and pleasure. It's been a dream of mine for many years. It's always been extremely important to me to let parents know that there is a legitimate, inexpensive way to get their children into show business. Now, hopefully, that message will get out!

You now have a basic understanding of what is expected of you and your child. You know what to do and how to do it, step by step. I told you it was going to be very simple. I also told you that I was going to be extremely honest with you, that I wasn't going to pull any punches. It *is* a long hard road, but an extremely rewarding one when your child makes it.

One of the most satisfying parts of my job is finding a child whom I feel has potential and creating a career for him or her. I love improving the quality of that child's life...and the life of his or her family. I wouldn't trade that—and the feeling I get from doing it—for all the money in Hollywood!

You Need To See The Truth Yourself

When I interview children, I always interview them for the first time in front of their parents. Many parents don't want me to do that. "My child performs so much better when I'm not around," they say. And they're right. So I always take into consideration that a child is sometimes inhibited by his parents. If, with the parent(s) right there, the child does extremely well, it definitely gives me a good indication that he or she would do even better alone.

Quite honestly, my reason for having the parent stay during our initial interview is not for the child, but for the parent. It will probably be the only time a parent is going to be able to see how her child auditions and handles interviews.

What would be the point of taking your child to meet an agent or a manager, waiting in the reception area, and then afterwards being told that he really needs some work in reading scripts or he doesn't really take direction well or "don't call us, we'll call you?" You may not be given any indication at all.

How can you ever figure out if all the time, travel and money you're investing is being well-spent?

The best way for you to see any of this—and believe me, you can tell—is to see it for yourself. During a typical 45-minute interview, I will do certain exercises with the child, and all of a sudden the mother will say to me, "I knew my child was talented. I knew my child was wonderful, but I had no idea that my child was capable of giving that type of performance. I had no idea that he was capable of expressing this type of emotion. I'm sitting here flabbergasted."

When I hear that, I know that my system of interviewing children in front of their parents is the right way to do it. I'm a parent myself. You have to know what is going on with your child. Anything else would be very frustrating.

I remember taking my own child to meet an agent, whom I knew. I was left in the reception area. When my daughter came out after the interview, I asked, "Well, how did she do?"

The answer was, "Well, you know, we're kind of busy now. We really can't let you know right now."

What do you *mean* you can't let me know right now? I had a feeling that they just didn't feel my child was ready to audition. If that were the case, then they should have simply told me.

Perhaps such experiences of my own have led to my emphasis on being "straight" with parents. I let them know right then and there if I think their child has potential. I let them know right then and there if I think the child is going to be extremely successful.

This is a big commitment, as I said before, and I don't want to fool anyone. I want you to know what it's like. That's what I've tried to get across in this book.

Don't Underestimate The Commitment

Everyone concerned has to take this seriously, which I expect you will now that you understand what is expected of you.

Several years ago, I interviewed a fourteen-year old girl. She assumed I ran a modeling agency. After several minutes of conversation I realized her mistake. I said, "I'm terribly sorry, but this is not a modeling agency. My clients are actors working in commercials, soaps, film, and Broadway. This is not the type of agency you should be looking for."

She looked at me, shrugged her shoulders, and said, "Okay, then I'll be an actress." It made me laugh. This is not the type of career you can take so lightly.

I remember another incident, involving a child around ten years old, who came highly recommended from a local

photographer. He called me and said, "You've got to see this
child. She's bright, she's outgoing, she's verbal."

When she got to *my* office, however, the little girl just sat
in a chair and refused to say a word to me. In fact, her hands
were folded across her chest the entire time. She was so
different from what the photographer said. I explained to the
mother that at the present time, there really wasn't much I
could do for her child. It was impossible for me to see her
child's potential.

Could you imagine, if this mother had been left out in the
reception area, her child behaved this way, and then I called
the mother in and I explained this to her. She would think I
was off the wall and probably say to me, "Well, that's not true.
The photographer said she was wonderful. She's always
performing, and blah, blah, blah."

This time, though, the mother said to me, "Oh, well, we
had an argument coming here, and my daughter is angry
with me."

Ah ha!

You know, it takes eight hours to shoot a thirty-second
commercial, and it costs hundreds of thousands of dollars.
Imagine a child sitting on the set, arms crossed, refusing to
say her lines! Obviously, that's not the type of child who would
be successful in this business. But the mother had to know
that—had to be *told* that—and I was very glad that I stuck
with my policy of interviewing children in front of their
parents.

It's very important for there to be a commitment on
everyone's part. If your child is no longer having fun doing
this, no longer *wants* to do it, stop! That's really my advice:
Stop! If you can keep your child interested, which I'm sure
you can, remember, show business is not the end-all and beall of life. Make it very light, make it fun, and you and your
child will be able to enjoy a fabulous career.

Let Me Hear From You!

I am so excited that the book is finished and that you've read it. I can't wait to hear from all of you. Please feel free to send me your comments on what you've read. I would love to hear about your experiences after you've gotten started. If you come across any other sources or local periodicals which might be of interest to other parents, please send them to me. Address all correspondence to:

Aggie Gold
Fresh Faces Management, Inc.
2911 Carnation Avenue
Baldwin, NY 11510

I want to take this opportunity to thank you for listening to me and for trusting my advice. And I want to wish you the very best luck.

As we say in the business, "Break a leg!"

Index